90 DAYS
TO SPARK YOUR
BEAUTY

IGNITE THE BEAUTY WITHIN!

A Devotional Journey

By

JILL WEATHERHEAD

To my amazing coach and friend Connie, Thank-you for believing in me and pulling me across the finish line. Can't wait for what's next. Love Jill

Copyright © 2022 Jill Weatherhead

Published by
Book Breakthrough Publishing, Surrey, UK

www.bookbreakthroughpublishing.com

All right reserved.
No part of this publication may be reproduced, distributed, or transmitted in any form or by any form including photocopying, recording, or other electronic or mechanical methods, without the prior written permission of the author and publisher, except in the case of brief quotations embodied in reviews and certain other noncommercial uses permitted by copyright law.

Holy Bible, New Living Translation, copyright © 1996, 2004, 2015 by Tyndale House Foundation. Tyndale House Publishers, Inc., Carol Stream, Illinois 60188. All rights reserved.

The Christian Standard Bible. Copyright © 2017 by Holman Bible Publishers. Christian Standard Bible®, and CSB® are federally registered trademarks of Holman Bible Publishers, all rights reserved.

The Holy Bible, English Standard Version. ESV®
Text Edition: 2016. Copyright © 2001
by Crossway Bibles, a publishing ministry of Good News Publishers.

ISBN: 978-1-9996790-4-0
Logo design: Alannah Lammiman

I AM A SPARK
by Sheila Brown

I am late, typically late
a natural born procrastinator.
I am a dreamer.
Which came first?
I wonder, how I got here and why?
I am a people pleaser, a server, a pacifist.
Sounds good, doesn't it?
Not so!
I am a disaster!
A people pleaser who cannot please enough,
A server who cannot serve enough,
A pacifist whose peace is hard fought.
I am tired and I am disillusioned.

But I have a friend,
She is a spark.
She is a spark who writes and paints and walks along the river.
She is a spark who loves a man and cooks and drinks fine wine.
She is a spark of resilience, a cheater of death, a traveller.
She is nice, a picture of kindness who looks after others.
And when I look really, really closely,
My friend, the spark
Looks a lot like me
I am a spark!

TABLE OF CONTENTS

Dedication .... **ix**

Acknowledgments .... **xi**

Introduction **1**

How to get the most from this 90-day journey **5**

Week 1: Starting the Journey **7**

   Day 1: Intro to the week – Who has the map? 9

   Day 2: My journey of discovery 11

   Day 3: What is beauty? 13

   Day 4: What beauty is not! 15

   Day 5: What do we think of ourselves when using the word beauty? 17

   Day 6: What does it take to create a 'spark' within us? 19

   Day 7: Time to go deeper – Journal Activity 21

Week 2: Getting Your House in Order **23**

   Day 8: Getting your house in order 25

   Day 9: Enter my house... you are welcome! 27

   Day 10: Kitchen or Dining Room? 29

   Day 11: The Bathroom 31

   Day 12: The Bedroom 33

   Day 13: Let's step back outside 35

   Day 14: Time to go deeper – Journal Activity 37

Week 3: Contrasts to consider 39
Day 15: Contrasts and Belief systems 41
Day 16: "Oh that's good. No that's bad." 43
Day 17: Are you too young or too old? 45
Day 18: Ugly vs Beautiful 47
Day 19: One size fits all 49
Day 20: Rich man – poor man 51
Day 21: Time to go deeper – Journal Activity 53

Week 4: Mindset 55
Day 22: It's all in my head 57
Day 23: Mind over matter 59
Day 24: I think I can!! 61
Day 25: Play it again Sam! 63
Day 26: Do you remember?? 65
Day 27: If only 67
Day 28: Time to go deeper – Journal Activity 69

Week 5: Interlude 71
Day 29: Uncommon commons 73
Day 30: Who am I? 75
Day 31: What makes me, me? 77
Day 32: Who do you say *I am*? 79
Day 33: Who do *you* say I am? 81
Day 34: The real you? 83
Day 35: Summary 85

Week 6: Culture and Beauty 87
Day 36: We are all the same? 89
Day 37: Fashion Culture 91
Day 38: And a one and a two… Fitness Culture 93
Day 39: Wellness Culture 95
Day 40: Family Culture 97

vi | Jill Weatherhead

Day 41: Diet Culture 99
Day 42: Time to go deeper – Journal Activity 101

Week 7: Who influences you? 103
Day 43: Influences from others: fictional or real 105
Day 44: A heroine from a book - Anne of Green Gables 107
Day 45: Do you have a Disney story favorite princess? 109
Day 46: Habits that are a result of influences 111
Day 47: What does it mean to be a woman? 113
Day 48: My Mother 115
Day 49: Time to go deeper – Journal Activity 117

Week 8: The various selfs 119
Day 50: What self is it that is you? 121
Day 51: What is my image of my 'self'? 123
Day 52: I think this, and so it is 125
Day 53: I see what I see... but I'd like to see 127
Day 54: What about my worth 129
Day 55: Self-confidence 131
Day 56: Time to go deeper – Journal Activity 133

Week 9: A Season of Giving 135
Day 57: From the inside out 137
Day 58: You've got mail!!! 139
Day 59: Who is calling? 141
Day 60: A daisy a day 143
Day 61: How are things in your corner of the world today? ... 145
Day 62: Paying it forward 147
Day 63: Time to go deeper - Journal Activity 149

Week 10: Time of celebration 151
Day 64: Take time to celebrate 153
Day 65: Happy birthday! 155
Day 66: Valentines Day 157

Day 67: Anniversary 159
Day 68: Mother's Day 161
Day 69: Christmas 163
Day 70: Time to go deeper – Journal Activity 165

Week 11: A new look... 167
Day 71: Out with the old – in with the new........................... 169
Day 72: Reflecting back.. 171
Day 73: Envision 173
Day 74: A new name 175
Day 75: New direction 177
Day 76: The purpose of life 179
Day 77: Time to go deeper - Journal Activity........................ 181

Week 12: Farming 183
Day 78: How does your garden grow?.................................. 185
Day 79: How to get started 187
Day 80: Preparing the garden 189
Day 81: Planting stage.. 191
Day 82: Now that the seed is sown what is next? 193
Day 83: Summer is here!... 195
Day 84: Time to go deeper - Journal Activity........................ 197

Week 13: Coming to the end 199
Day 85: Coming to the end of the journey 201
Day 86: A distance traveled 203
Day 87: Come out from hiding.. 205
Day 88: Beauty with confidence 207
Day 89: Have you seen the sunrise?.................................... 209
Day 90: Hello everyone! I'm home!..................................... 211

This is not the end - it is in fact a new beginning 213

About the Author 215

DEDICATION

To the memory of Katrina Suzanne McGillivray

January 13, 1960 - November 4, 2021

She fought the good fight with a smile and grace and love for everyone she met.

ACKNOWLEDGMENTS

There are so many people to say thank you in helping me have this book become a reality. To list them all would mean another book. Thank you to all of you who have prayed for me during the editing of the book. Thank you to the various counsellors and coaches over the years that have helped me get that one step farther in the journey of believing in true beauty.

To my publisher Sue who said without one minute of doubt that I could write this book.

To three very special women who have known me for many years, and yet still we are friends – Deb M, Pam L, Maureen J.

Jennifer Trask, who told me not what I wanted to hear but what I needed to hear and who opened my eyes to what my soul already knew existed.

My sister, Rosanne, who has been more than a sister over the years but has been the mother when our mother was unable to care for me, and the cheerleader believing I could do anything.

My sons Eric & Glen who walked a lot of the ugly part of this journey and continued to love and forgive me. To my daughter in laws, Esther and Stacy for being patient with me as I learn to accept all our unique ways of seeing the world. And to my grandchildren:

Kylie, Kenzie (Mackenzie), Luana, Kodie (Dakota) and Marcus who make me want to be the best Nana in the world.

My partner, my best friend and the one who told me that he did not marry me for my looks because that was not what was beautiful about me. Dr. Norm you continue to care, love and inspire me to be authentically me. You spark my beauty – inside and out!

INTRODUCTION

*H*ave you ever found yourself struggling to see beauty in you? Have you desired to have a greater sense of self-worth?

When did the idea really 'spark'? What does it even mean to "spark your beauty"?

There have been phases I believe throughout my life that I have struggled with the simple act of looking in the mirror. I mean really looking. And looking with love and acceptance at what I see.

I know there have been times in my life that I have struggled to feel worthy. To be able to love myself. Most of my life has been about serving others. I have also struggled with being me. The real me.

The world was in dread at what was happening globally with something unknown and spreading rapidly. In history books, now it will be referred to as the global pandemic of 2020. In this midst of this, I was looking for something to lift my spirits and I washed my hair. A friend, Stephanie Grove, had given me samples to try something new. It sounds simple, doesn't it? And yet that was like a spark as this new shampoo brand made my hair feel so amazing that I felt a sense of beauty.

This little spark has now grown and led me to have a vision and a mission to help other women truly see their beauty.

You see I believe that we are all created beautiful.

> "God saw all that he had made,
> and it was very good indeed."
> Genesis 1:31 (CSB)

Also I believe that we all hold this belief at the beginning of life. However, for some of us, at some point in our life, someone says something, or some event happens, and we lose touch with that belief.

But a turning point came for me when my dear friend died.

Katrina (to whom the book is dedicated) loved unconditionally. She saw the good in people. I was her best friend. And yet, if you knew her personally you might argue with me and say that you were her best friend. And yes, we would both be correct. That was Katrina. That was how she loved.

You see she had a beautiful soul. Even up to the very end, she smiled as she lay in a coma with the cancer fight almost over. She smiled as her family sang to her, prayed with her, told her they would miss her.

I fell into a depression after her death. The global strife – the division of families and churches and workplaces over policies to protect the population – made everywhere I looked very grey. I struggled to see any beauty.

But at my darkest point, a small flicker began, another spark even, and a Facebook challenge was created. I set it up to be 90 days to talk about beauty. The idea was that each day I would post and ponder with those who joined me to see what we could determine: Why are there people like me who feel they don't have 'beauty'?

Through that Facebook 90-day writing, this book truly came to life. I want to tell my story and hope that others (like you) who read this book will once again be able to look up and see the beauty. To be able to look in the mirror and see the light that shines deep within.

So, my mission, my dream, my desire, is to help to spark your inner beauty! Read on to see how you can do that.

I've created a guide to help you to know how to get the most from this journey. And I believe that if you stay with me, by the end of the 90 days you too can look in the mirror and see the real beautiful you!

Our goal together is to find that beauty which lies within and let it be ignited and shine brightly. Be the you that you were created to be! Together we can make this world beautiful again.

Together we can say like God did in Genesis, *"And he looked at all he created and said, 'It is very good!'"*

HOW TO GET THE MOST FROM THIS 90-DAY JOURNEY

The pages ahead are full of examples of my journey and a bit of my story. Some of what is written will be easy to read. Some might be harder. It all depends on where you are in your journey of being you – the real you God created you to be.

For the most part you will want to do the chapters in the order they are written as the intent was that we discover and grow along the road to the 90th day.

Each week will start with the first day being an introduction to the theme of the week. Then there will be five days of content relevant to the week's theme with each day ending with a "Thought to Ponder". The seventh day will be an exercise to "Go Deeper" on the topic. It is up to you to journal each day as you complete it or to journal just once a week on the discoveries you are making.

Before you start each day's reading, take some time to pray in preparation. Ask Holy Spirit to guide your thoughts and to protect your heart.

I want you to know this is a self-paced book. It was designed as a 90-day journey, but you may need more or less time. Take the time you need to let the contents of each day and the topic theme of the week sink in and take time to reflect on what you learn as you go along.

Some of the days might make you need to stop and pause before just reading on. If you feel prompted to do so, please take some time. If you feel resistance, again take some time to journal and pray to discern where the resistance is coming from.

A disclaimer here: I am not a professional therapist. This journey is mine and the discoveries are mine. I do admit that some of the days took me to a deeper darkness before I could find the light again. If you find that is happening to you, put the book down, pick up your phone and call someone. You may need some professional help to guide you through some of what you start understanding about yourself.

Above all claim this promise from Romans 8:35-38

> [35] *Can anything ever separate us from Christ's love? Does it mean he no longer loves us if we have trouble or calamity, or are persecuted, or hungry, or destitute, or in danger, or threatened with death?*
>
> [37] *No, despite all these things, overwhelming victory is ours through Christ, who loved us.*
>
> [38] *And I am convinced that **nothing** can ever separate us from God's love. (NLT)*

Are you ready? Then let's start this journey, shall we?

Week 1

STARTING THE JOURNEY

*"The heart of man plans his way,
but the Lord establishes his steps."
Proverbs 16:9 (ESV)*

Day 1

INTRO TO THE WEEK – WHO HAS THE MAP?

Welcome to week 1 of a journey towards "sparking your beauty"! I am so glad you are here with me. Each week will start with an introduction to the topic of the week. There will also be a scripture focus to help us remember that we are not on this journey alone.

As with any journey, it is important to have a map. A plan. An idea of where you would like to go. If it is true that life is about the journey more than the destination, then it is important for you to take a moment to note where you are in your present self-discovery journey. Throughout the days ahead the question of who has the map will have different answers as you will see. For the most part I have created a map – an outline of a journey I took and the places along the way that needed some time to stop, reflect, and make changes before moving on.

On this journey with me, you may find some of your beliefs challenged. Some discoveries will be new. Some will be building blocks on previous growth spurts. So, let's first take some time to consider what we think at the start of these 90 days together concerning:

*What is beauty?

*What beauty is not?

*What we think about ourselves when we use the word 'beauty'?

*What will it take to "spark your beauty"?

From experience, I can tell you that when you start a journey, there will always be events that will be like roadblocks and detours and delays, and you may even discover the desire to quit. I will be praying for you that you will continue to the end.

Thought to ponder

With any plans you make, take a moment to pray and ask Holy Spirit to help guide you in this 90-day process. Write down two or three ideas you hope to explore as we journey together.

Day 2

MY JOURNEY OF DISCOVERY

The road map I am using is based on my own journey that to date has spanned more than six decades. In my over 60 years, I have traveled a great deal and moved frequently. In some ways that has helped speed up certain stages of my personal growth, but it also created some roadblocks, closed roads, detours and yes, even my desire a few times to get off the journey completely. To take a short cut and just be in Heaven. But I persevere thanks be to God.

As an experienced global traveler, I know whenever I am planning a trip that one of the important factors to determine is how much time I want to spend in getting to the destination.

In our early years of marriage, it was pre-GPS era and the route was planned by studying a paper map. Our first big trip was from Calgary Alberta to Port Arthur, Texas. We had studied and planned how long we would drive each day and the plan was to put up a tent and camp each night. I was going to be starting a nursing job in Texas and we had a week to make the drive.

My husband was the primary driver, so it was up to me to read the map. Did I mention that prior to this trip and even now I may be a little direction challenged? Driving on interstates was different too and knowing ahead of time the exit we were to take, was often necessary to prevent extra miles of driving.

I'm sure you are smiling or at least already guessing it took a few missed exits before I felt more confident in giving him directions. We did make is safely to our destination. Not in the time frame we had planned and that is due in part to what I want to remind you and me as we journey together.

We can set out with our plans. But sometimes things do not go the way we had thought. An intense rainstorm prevented one night of camping, but we are thankful for the hotel room that was provided. And that is the part of this journey I want us to remember.

The verse for this week is to remind us that while we make our plans, we need to be sure to consult God and listen closely to His direction. The "map" you end up drawing for yourself may end up having some different turns and changes to what your original thought was at the start of this journey.

Thought to ponder

Spend some time today to consider who is holding your map. Are you open to God leading and having full control in all areas of your life?

Day 3

WHAT IS BEAUTY?

It is said that "Beauty is in the eye of the beholder." (Margaret Wolfe Hungerford) If we agree and believe this statement, then it puts the 'power' of beauty back into our hands (or minds and hearts).

There is much written on the various aspects of beauty that it would be too much for the purpose of today. But it is a starting point for you as you think about your own definition. In my creation of my blog (sparkyrbeauty.com), I do an exercise where I first ask the reader to close their eyes and picture the word "beauty". At the end of this week, I have created a few exercises for you as you take note of what you believe at the start of this journey.

For me it was a struggle to think of myself as beautiful for various reasons that will be talked about in future weeks. I still have my moments when I cannot look at myself in the mirror. More recently it has been more difficult to hear people call me beautiful.

Since it is a concept that I struggled with in my own self-image, I decided to look at photos and determine which ones I liked of myself. After randomly choosing 10 pictures, the common factor seemed that there was a glow or a sparkle in my eyes, not just a smile on my face. These photos were the ones where I felt that yes, I liked the photo. Interestingly, one photo is of me at the end of a difficult bike ride. My hair is messy, I am all sweaty. Yet the exhilaration of completing a difficult training ride and the sweet comment by the photographer combined to create this belief that I was beautiful in that moment. Our wedding day was another photo that brings a smile to my lips. As well as on our 30th wedding anniversary when we renewed our vows on the beach in Cancun and had our grown children as witnesses, even while the storm threatened to pour rain on us. But beauty is more than just how you look in a photo.

In future weeks, I will share more about my thoughts on what will bring about a spark of beauty within you. I will also share my journey of what misbeliefs and influences in my life have blocked that beauty and light from shining.

> **Thought to ponder**
> What is the beauty you see in your favorite photograph or picture of yourself?

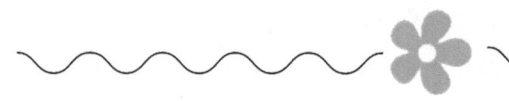

Day 4

WHAT BEAUTY IS NOT!

In Romeo and Juliet, Shakespeare coins the phrase, "a rose by any other name would smell as sweet." If I have determined that beauty is the inner being that shines from the inside out, then beauty is not something just on the outside.

For the purposes of this journey, I would like to suggest that beauty is not JUST the outer person. Often it is the accessories that bring out that beauty as a person may feel more confident as they wear certain clothing, or add some jewelry, or use highlighting with makeup on. We will look at this deeper in the chapter on culture, but I just want to plant the seed now that accessories of beauty also may include our quality traits — consider what is said in Galatians 5.

Going back to the photos, it is also those who may be around us when the picture is being taken or the event that happened which brings this light to our eyes, and we shine to the world around us.

If we take nature as our example, we do see how our senses light up to certain vision arounds us. Living near the Rocky Mountains, I have the opportunity to see a variety of accessories that makes one mountain stand out as more 'beautiful' than perhaps the others. One of my favorites is a mountain that has snow on it all year round. It also has waterfalls throughout the year at various heights.

These contrasts lend a beauty to this mountain such that it is very frequently photographed by many people.

As humans, we have more accessories than just the clothing and jewelry that we wear. In fact, I believe that it is our accessories that add to or detract from our personality traits. These can heighten the goodness of a person's soul and therefore add to their beauty. I believe that is what is meant when they say, 'love is blind'. When you love someone, you may have more difficulty separating the physical attributes of that person from their personality, and therefore, it is your love that helps you look at and see that person as beautiful.

> **Thought to ponder**
>
> Take some time to read Galatians 5:22-23. Then ponder what accessories you feel are important to make you believe in your own beauty?

Day 5

WHAT DO WE THINK OF OURSELVES WHEN USING THE WORD BEAUTY?

———————

This may be where the rubber hits the road in our journey. For too many of us, it is easy to look at others and to see beauty. It may be easy to look at a flower garden, a flowing river, a newborn baby, or a bride. These give us a sense of knowing what beauty is.

But can we see the beauty in ourselves? Growing up I was taught it was vain if I said or thought of myself as beautiful. Have you heard of the amazing woman of Proverbs 31 in the Bible? She had many positive qualities mentioned, but notice what this one line says, "Charm is deceitful, beauty is fleeting, but the woman who fears the Lord is to be praised."

On the one hand, we should not be gazing into the mirror wondering if we are the fairest of them all like in the fairy tales of old.

On the other hand, we are to recognize that we have all been created beautiful.

We will look at this in more depth later. For now, I think of when I look at myself in the mirror. Do I see the beauty? Or do I see the flaws in the reflection? When I interact with others and show grace, mercy, and love, is it then that I am beautiful?

There are women in the Bible who are listed as being beautiful. There are many passages that talk about the ideas around beauty – for better and worse. I will be using some of these throughout the 90 days but there will be time to go deeper at the end of this week.

> ### Thought to ponder
>
> Before going much further, take a moment to evaluate your response to the idea that "we are all created beautiful". Do you agree or disagree that we are all created beautiful?

Day 6

WHAT DOES IT TAKE TO CREATE A 'SPARK' WITHIN US?

When I was a child, a spark would be lit with just two words, "Daddy's home!" It was the high point of my day. I am so thankful to have had a father who I know really loved me. Past tense? Yes, he died suddenly when I was only 10 years old. According to my sister, I was the apple of his eye. That is indeed a treasure I keep close in my heart.

My point is that there was a moment when I knew there was a spark. Followed by a smile and the heart-warming hug that would follow. Even replaying the memory in my mind has a similar response.

I have been loved in my life by others. Family, friends, my husband, my children, and now my grandchildren. Now hearing "Hi Nana" from my granddaughters has the similar affect on me as my initial feelings about myself all those years ago with my father.

Briefly, I just want to say, I believe that when we are at our peak performance, however that looks, then we can more clearly see this 'beauty' that we are talking about. I also believe that when we feel we are true to ourselves that there is a little spark inside that reminds us of our true value. Our worth.

In the same way that I believe we are all beautiful, I also believe that we are all worthy. Not for any other reason than just the fact that we exist. That we were created. Later in this journey we will spend more time on this topic but for now, another seed – I am worthy. You are worthy.

I love to hear, "Welcome, we're glad you are here". There is a sense of belonging, importance, value. When we are happy in any given moment, there is a physical response to that akin to a beauty and a spark. Or what about in those special moments when you can actually feel God's presence? There is often an emotional response as well.

We will look at contrasts in a few weeks, but for this moment, I want us to also consider the ways our fire dims. Like those times when we don't feel loved, worthy, or socially acceptable. Emotionally we curl up - this is where I feel I am most weak. My emotions are still affected by my environment. This is one area where I am still learning, growing, and changing. A rejection from someone still sends me to want to curl up somewhere.

From the spark a flame can grow, and we can then be a light to others. Wouldn't it be great to become not just a spark but a flame and a roaring fire that no one and nothing can put out?

> **Thought to ponder**
>
> What are some of the things that come to mind as you consider what 'sparks' your beauty?

Day 7

TIME TO GO DEEPER
JOURNAL ACTIVITY

At the end of every week, I want you to take some time to not just ponder but to reflect on the topics of the week. Take some time to go back to the daily notes you have made and see if there are thoughts you need to spend more time in prayer asking God for help.

At the end of each week there will be exercises and scriptures for you to be able to go deeper in this journey in getting your spark ignited.

Today I want you to do these five tasks to get a response from your senses as you work on your definitions, beliefs, and understanding when it comes to beauty:

1. Sight - Look in the mirror for the first task. As you gaze for a few minutes, see if you can identify one aspect of what you are seeing as beautiful.

2. Feel – Go outside. Is there a breeze? Does it lift the hair away from your face? Is there sunshine? Do you feel the warmth on your skin? If it is still winter, do you feel the chill in a way that is actually refreshing?

3. Taste - Eat something you like. Did you choose something sweet? Sour? What is the sensation as the flavor moves around in your mouth?

4. Hear - Listen to a piece of music. What stirs within you as you listen? Is there a smile on your face? Or a tear creeping down your cheek? Or do you simply want to get up and dance?

5. Smell - Find something that your nose says is 'beautiful'. How did your nose and brain decide it was beautiful?

"Humans do not see what the LORD sees, for humans see what is visible, but the LORD sees the heart."
1 Samuel 16:7b (CSB)

Week 2

GETTING YOUR HOUSE IN ORDER

*"Do you not know that you are
God's temple and that God's Spirit dwells in you?
If anyone destroys God's temple, God will destroy him.
For God's temple is holy, and you are that temple."
1 Corinthians 3:16-17 (ESV))*

Day 8

GETTING YOUR HOUSE IN ORDER

One of the things that my mom struggled with as she was teaching me life skills was that I was always messy. She often would open the door to my room and sigh, "How do you find anything in this mess?" Then she would walk away, shaking her head as she went.

For my mom, a messy room equated a messy life. It made statements about values I did not realize I was lacking, or perhaps it was that I had a different viewpoint. She also felt that one day when I got my own place, things would be different. At least we agreed on that point.

The first place I lived at away from home was a shared room in a dorm at college. My roommate took on the same view as my mother. There was a place for everything, and everything had its place. My brain would not accept this, and it was a very long year for the both of us. It is not surprising that I married a man with these ideals as well.

When I started creating this 90-day journey, the one thing I concluded was that I was not a messy person. It was just not a priority to have things in 'their place'. My ideal place is one that has comfort mixed with cleanliness. I do notice a parallel though, as I want to be the best 'me' and that is what I need to get my house in 'order' – however I choose to define what that looks like while walking in prayer.

Leading in then to the focus of this week, we are going to look metaphorically at getting our house in order. To do that we are going to go through each room of a typical house and see what we learn about ourselves. While I want you to reflect on the parallel, I want you to look at your present dwelling place as well as we go through each of the rooms. Perhaps you already know some areas that 'need work'.

> ### Thought to ponder
> How do you think the way your keep your house (your literal house as well as your 'temple' body) affects your 'spark'? Are there ways you see that it impacts on how you show up in daily life?

Day 9

ENTER MY HOUSE...
YOU ARE WELCOME!

When your friends or family come over to visit, do you open the door wide and help them into your front room? Or do you hold back a little for a few minutes?

Growing up in the Maritime region of Canada, my relatives had a room they called the parlour. As a child, if I was allowed into that room, I had to be very careful to not touch anything. I remember the chairs were not very comfortable and I could not really understand the purpose of this room. This was a very formal sitting area. I did not feel welcome in this room although all the objects were very pretty antiques.

As time went by, I noticed a pattern. Not everyone invited you into their parlor. In fact, those who were closer friends with my parents would invite us into a different area. It was cozy and comfortable and felt like 'home'. Quite often it was called the 'den' or family room or even living room. I found these rooms easier to be in with these people, and even found myself much more relaxed and not as stressed about being myself.

In your evaluation of your practices, what does this room say about you? Or is your welcome based on who the person is that you are inviting into your home?

Presently we are in a small, albeit mostly comfortable, basement suite. By design if I invite you in, you will find yourself in my living room. I will admit that I do not feel comfortable hosting people in this new place for fear of judgement at what people will say about what they see.

Taking the picture then of our living room and my feelings about where I live, I recognize that I can be the same when I deal with people. Those with whom I feel secure in my relationship have been invited in, offered a place to sit and to stay awhile.

> **Thought to ponder**
>
> As we look at 'sparking beauty', take some time to look at this room in your physical house as well as the idea of opening up your life to others. How does your house affect your 'spark'?

Day 10

KITCHEN OR DINING ROOM?

Where do you find the most action in your home? The best conversations?

There are two points here as we look at kitchen and dining room. One is how open are we to receive people - the gift of hospitality. The second is how we relate to others – openness, yes but with humility.

The kitchen for me over the years has been a place I much enjoy. I need to preface this to say I am an extrovert, so being with others is a true joy. I have lots of memories of laughter and natural conversations which happened when we were preparing a meal with extended family or friends as well as during the clean up time afterwards.

If I could design my perfect house, it would certainly be with an open kitchen into the dining room. And it would have space for 'bar stools' so the guests could just sit and chat with me while I prepared a meal.

When we come together as a family for special occasions at either of my son's homes, when it comes time to eat, we do sit at the dining room table. The introverts of the family feel more comfortable here as the extroverts entertain. It also allows time for the introverts to feel relaxed and may even join in on the conversations.

The dining room table is not just for food sharing. It is a place that can be a place of fellowship. Is there anything more beautiful than the picture of laugher, sharing stories, and community feasting around a table?

Thought to ponder

Take some time to find scriptures that talk about the importance of hospitality to others. Read Luke 13:29-30 and discover the hospitality of God that is available to all and the great banquet that is to come.

Day 11

THE BATHROOM

Did you grow up with the saying: "Cleanliness is next to Godliness"? The bathroom is often the room I make sure is the cleanest (well, next to the kitchen sink).

The bathroom – this is a place that may also reveal a lot about us. We only have one bathroom where we live now, but in other houses we also had a 'guest' bathroom. It was decorated differently - the towels were neatly folded, and there was always more than enough toilet paper and Kleenex available in it. It had various decorations and of course some scented mist in case of odor. I did all this to make sure a visitor to my home felt comfortable.

In the last place we lived, we built an ensuite bathroom to our bedroom. It was my favorite bathroom in all the places we had lived, mostly because I had a say in how it was designed. I had always dreamed of having a large walk-in shower with one of the shower heads being a waterfall shower. This was my 'retreat' area, a place I went to when I wanted to run away from it all. I know a lot of people like a bath, but there is something special to me about rinsing off in a shower that feels like all my cares are being washed away.

Today, my place only has a cubicle bathroom shower that is built tall and is very narrow (or maybe it is just I am larger?). I miss my waterfall experience.

While I am not one to spend time looking in the mirror, I do appreciate a bathroom that gives me a good overall view of my reflection. For years, it was more a judgement than an acceptance activity. I would look myself over to make sure I was presentable to the outside world. It is only more recently that I have found it gives me a sense of pleasure to see my reflection. Now, instead of the judgement, I give myself a smile and a 'high five' as I head out for the day or as I head to bed. This has become a part of accepting myself.

> **Thought to ponder**
>
> If you only have one bathroom in your house, is it decorated with you in mind, or do you keep it to some higher standard in case company comes?

Day 12

THE BEDROOM

---

*I*ntimacy...retreat...privacy - those are just some words that come to mind when I think of the bedroom in my 'house'.

Sleep is important for our health and overall beauty. Did you know that for most of us we spend more than 1/3 of our lives in this room?

One of the "must have" items for me is to have a window where I can lay in bed and look outside and see the sky. I have told both my husband and my sons that this is an important factor for the day that I go into a nursing home, should that be in my future. It is that important to me.

At the time of writing this book, we are living in a basement suite. In fact, we have been living in a basement suite for more years than I would have chosen to do. So yes, I dream of a new house some day that is above ground. I'm not completely sure which of the rooms in our place is my favorite but I do love the bedroom. It has the blessing of having the largest window and the amount of natural sunlight coming in is high all year long. I must admit that some days I love to just lay in bed and look at the sky. When the weather permits, I love to have the window open and listen to birds singing in the early morning.

I would have to say that for me I am willing to share my entire house with you – except this one room. It is my most private place.

> **Thought to ponder**
>
> Is your bedroom your place of rest? A place to retreat? What are some things you have that help with making it an oasis?

Day 13

LET'S STEP BACK OUTSIDE

Do you have a porch? A balcony? A deck? One of my favorite styles of houses is one that has a front porch. Growing up, we moved a lot with my dad being in the Air Force. I had an aunt and uncle who lived in the same place for all those years, and they had a front room off the parlor that was the 'sunroom'. This enclosed room was a place for reading and daydreaming which I did a lot of when I stayed with them.

As an adult, I would visit another aunt and uncle who had a front porch with a swing. Three people could sit on it comfortably. There was something very welcoming about driving up to their house and seeing my aunt on the porch waving us hello and then when we left, her waving goodbye.

The more popular outside addition to a house now it seems is to have a deck. It is usually in the backyard and considered to be a more private place. One of the blessings of our present place is the open heart of our landlady who lets us enjoy her backyard as if it was our own. This makes summer entertaining so much easier. During the times of pandemic restrictions, it was certainly a blessing to have the wide-open space that our family could gather. One daughter-in-law and her three girls often drop by on their way home from being 'south' in the city. We have a snack and then the three run off to play.

For most of the year, I go and sit on the chairs on the deck. It gets the full sun and very little wind. It's a lovely place to just sit and be still. Sip my coffee. Read a book. Or do some writing. During the lockdown of 2020, it was strange to hear the stillness. No planes. No traffic. Only the birds were heard and the occasional bark of the neighbors' dogs. Now when I sit out there, you can hear the activity of the city - planes overhead and the hum of the traffic on the main traffic artery about 4 kms away. I find peace in both, and I have to say that I also enjoy the privacy this backyard gives me.

Thought to ponder

Which would be your preference – to be open on the front porch and watch the world going by? Or to sit in the back deck area and be more private? What do you think this says about you and your relationship to those around you?

Day 14

TIME TO GO DEEPER
JOURNAL ACTIVITY

"Everyone then who hears these words of mine and does them will be like a wise man who built his house on the rock. And the rain fell, and the floods came, and the winds blew and beat on that house, but it did not fall, because it had been founded on the rock." Matthew 7:24-25(CSB)

The purpose of this week was to walk through your physical dwelling and to think of how each room tells a story about you. I want you to take some time to go deeper and use the following thoughts to prompt your journal activity.

As you consider your present dwelling place, take some time to discern which room brings you the most joy? What it is about this room that you love so much?

In contrast, what is the one room that never seems to measure up to your heart's desire?

Where do you feel most safe? Where do you feel more judged or vulnerable? Where it is totally private?

How does all this fit with this journey we are on in discovering and redefining 'beauty'?

> **Read – Reflect – Pray**
> Psalm 84; John 14:2; Hebrews 3:6

Week 3

CONTRASTS TO CONSIDER

*"For he makes his sun rise on
the evil and on the good and sends rain
on the just and on the unjust."*
Matthew 5:45b (CSB)

Day 15

CONTRASTS AND BELIEF SYSTEMS

---

*H*ave you read thru the first part of Ecclesiastes? It starts out listing a long list of contrasts – opposites in a sense. One of the more famous writers that used contrasts was Charles Dickens and you may recognize this section from the Tale of Two Cities:

> It was the best of times, it was the worst of times, it was the age of wisdom, it was the age of foolishness, it was the epoch of belief, it was the epoch of incredulity, it was the season of Light, it was the season of Darkness, it was the spring of hope, it was the winter of despair, we had everything before us, we had nothing before us.

But the writer of Ecclesiastes goes on further to talk about contrasts by concluding that there is a season – a time - for every matter under heaven (3:1) and follows with a list: born/die; plant/reap; kill/heal/ break down/build up; weep/laugh; mourn/dance; cast away stones/gather stones; embrace/refrain from embracing; seek/lose; keep/cast away; tear/sew; keep silence/speak; love/hate; war/peace. (Ecclesiastes 3:2-8).

As a woman, I feel that as my hormones shift through the seasons, I can find myself and the view of myself strongly affected, either negatively pulling me into darkness or bringing me back to the light.

This week I want to look at some of the contrasts that I believe have led me to some of my beliefs about who am I and my worth. Some of these help my light to shine but some have caused me to withdraw and hide my light in safety. Overall though I do know that I am a work in progress.

> **Thought to ponder**
>
> How do you feel your beauty has been affected by the various seasons of life? Knowing that life has seasons, what comfort can we find in Philippians 1:6?

Day 16

"OH THAT'S GOOD. NO THAT'S BAD."

A contrast does not necessarily mean an opposite of something, although that is the belief usually held by many people. To examine this, let's begin by considering the most common of contrasts – good vs bad.

One of my favorite jokes growing up was one my dad would tell. I called it, "Oh that's good. No that's bad". It is a long joke, so I will only give you a few lines for you to get the gist of it.

> M: My friend fell out of an airplane.   Y: *Oh, that's bad.*
>
> M: No, that's not bad, that's good. He was wearing a parachute.   Y: *Oh, that's good.*
>
> M: No, that's bad. His parachute would not open.   Y: *Oh, that's bad.*
>
> M: No, it's not bad. It's good. He fell into a large haystack.   Y: *Oh, that's good.*

The joke goes on, but I think you get the idea.

The point I want to make here is that how we determine or believe something is good or bad can often be related to the facts we have or perhaps do not have. Falling out of a plane is certainly bad if that is all you knew. But then knowing he had a parachute, your position statement changed, and it was 'good'.

Growing up I was a 'good girl' if I did certain behaviors and a 'bad' girl if I did other behaviors. A seed of belief was then planted in me that if I wanted approval I needed to behave in a certain way and within certain parameters. My self judgement was often the more difficult task master than any one person trying to help me to improve. This voice inside is often an inner critic built on untruths about who I truly am. We will look more at this in coming chapters, but it is important that we acknowledge what we may be saying to ourselves that affect how we begin to see ourselves.

In raising my sons, I wanted to focus more on the activity that was approved or not necessarily approved, rather than use the idea of 'bad/good'. I am not sure I was always successful. I am proud of the men they are today. Now as a grandmother, I find that we have longer discussions about acceptable behaviours and those deemed as 'unacceptable'. It gets a little more confusing sometimes since what I feel about certain things may differ from the parents' point of view. Nonetheless, how we are disciplined and what we believe as we grow up has an impact on whether we feel open to shine and to be our true selves or not.

> **Thought to ponder**
>
> How do you feel the way you were brought up has affected your inner 'spark'? Do you have days that your inner critique takes over in your thoughts about who you are? What truths do we know from God's word when it comes to our value?

Day 17

ARE YOU TOO YOUNG OR TOO OLD?

Another contrast is related to the age we find ourselves and the words 'young' vs 'old'.

I am the youngest of four children so I will always be considered 'the baby'. I watched as my three siblings were allowed to do things I was not and when I asked why, the answer was more commonly "you are too young."

I call my youngest son my baby (which his daughter thinks is very funny) because he is my last- born. My eldest granddaughter, who was six at the time, told me that I was too old to be on the swings. When she saw me make a sad face she quickly added, "But Nana, you are not as old as the dinosaurs!" I believe her comment was intended to make me smile, which it did.

The labels we give for various stages in life also shape how we look at each other: Newborn, Toddler, Preschooler, School Age, Teenager, Young Adult, Middle Adult, Senior Citizen. After that I guess you are just 'older'.

With each of these stages of life also come expectations on what we are doing, who we are doing it with, and how we should act. My youngest grandchild crying because he is hungry is acceptable since that is the only way he can communicate his needs. As an 'older' adult, it would not be accepted in our society if I cried in the same manner when we go out to eat and the food was not ready when my stomach was growling.

As one who has traveled and lived in a few different countries and cultures, what I have learned is that the given categorized list of 'stages' is very Canadian. For example, in the village where we spent some time in Papua New Guinea, anyone over 40 was an 'old' person. The media here at home in Canada now talks about 60 being the new 40, and 50 being the new 30.

> **Thought to ponder**
>
> What are some of the positives of the stage of life you find yourself in at this moment? What does God's Word teach us about seasons of life in relation to beauty?

Day 18

UGLY VS BEAUTIFUL

Are you familiar with the story of *"The Ugly Duckling"*? If not, take the time to read it. Even if you have read it many times, may I suggest you read it again with the thoughts we are looking at and considering together in this 90-day journey.

I remember the first time I read it. I remember the impact it had on me. Sometimes we just do not feel like we fit in to the crowd of people around us. That can have such an impact on how we see ourselves.

What were some of the reasons the 'duckling' felt 'ugly'?

The comparison trap would be my first thought. The opinions of others also factored in. But really, the biggest problem for him was how he saw himself – ugly. It did not help that others around fed into this belief so much so that he went away to be on his own.

I believe there are stages of our lives when we do not feel as attractive as we might like to be. The problem is that if we continue to use harmful self-talk, then we end up creating a misbelief about ourselves. I am not sure of this, but I do believe that for many there is a period of time where we just don't feel like we fit into our own skin, let alone fit in among others.

As I headed into my teen years, it would have been good to have kept those thoughts in focus, but I am afraid I did not. I did get caught up in the comparison trap and still struggle with this at times. One of the hardest things for me is being able to look in the mirror and see myself. No judgement. Just a long hard look.

> **Thought to ponder**
>
> When you look at yourself in the mirror or in pictures, what do you see? How do you determine if you are beautiful or ugly? Is your answer based on the comparison like the swan did in his/her early stage of life? Take time to meditate on Psalm 139 to help soak in the truth found in verse 14 that we are 'wonderfully made'.

Day 19

ONE SIZE FITS ALL

I am not a fan of shopping for clothing for many reasons. But I find it interesting how many 'scales' we have that measure and put us in groups. We will look at this more in a future chapter when we talk about our self-image, but for now I just want to talk about the contrasts and the beliefs that are created with them.

There was a time when my sister and I could almost wear the same clothing. It was not a very long period because I have a bigger build and she has a smaller build. I do remember that one shirt of hers that I wore once made me feel all beautiful and sexy. I hoped that by wearing it, that I too could be attractive to the boys like she was.

I still remember one of the times too when one of her boyfriends came to pick her up and we had a dog who went charging at him. I can still hear him saying, "Oh I didn't know you had an older sister." This young man was quickly ushered out the door by my sister, but I stood there pleased to be 4 inches taller at that time and had for one moment been the 'older sister'.

It is not completely your 'fault' that you have these feelings about your body image, however. Right from the first time we are weighed and measured at birth, we are then evaluated by a chart that dictates if we are small, average, or large. Further evaluations in our first year of life plot us on a graph that will say we are in a specific percentile. Then we go to school, and we quickly learn that if you are an A student, that is above average, and a B student might be average, but certainly a C student is not academically inclined.

From my years of working as a nurse, I can tell you that the grades I had in nursing school were not part of me being hired. Nor did the patient I was caring for ask to see those credentials. I did pass my RN exams quite well, I have to admit. One of my friends passed by only 30 points above the passing grade. But to see us working side-by-side, you would not know there was a difference. Perhaps I felt more confidence because of my higher grade? Or perhaps just knowing I had passed a difficult exam gave me that confidence.

So, these evaluations of our self do affect our inner beauty as we either will stand tall with confidence in knowing what our talents and abilities are, or we will hold back, not really self-actualizing, and in fact letting the light inside us be hidden from the world. Self worth will be discussed in detail in a few chapters but for now keep in mind that we are all worthy because we are human beings. All of us are loved by God who created us in His image.

Thought to ponder

How do you feel your 'size' affects how you feel about your beauty? Are these the measurements you use to create your sense of worth? What talents make you feel 'bigger than life'? Spend some time thinking about the gifts and talents God has given you.

Day 20

RICH MAN – POOR MAN

I left this contrast to the end of the week because I wanted to give you time to think through the others before tomorrow when you take the time to go deeper. The first step in this contrast is based on how we define what is rich and what is poor.

The Bible has a lot of examples of rich and poor and for the most part when we talk about it, we think about it from a monetary and/or material possessions perspective. For me, that is how I have held beliefs about these two words – until more recently.

In the chapters ahead we will look more into the comparison trap, but for now let me say that I believe how we define these words and how we assess ourselves is often done by comparing to standards that we learn as we journey through life.

During the years of living in a developing country, I felt rich in comparison to those around me. If for no other reason than if a need arose, we had the ability to reach out to get assistance. Those in the village around us in Papua New Guinea were subsistence famers and relied on their jungle garden crop to be their source of food.

But something changed about the time when my 'beauty' was sparked. My eyes were opened to possibilities that I had not yet discovered. What if abundance meant something else entirely?

It became even more clear to me when I was in an interview. As I explained this new way of thinking, I had an epiphany moment.

While it is true there is a monetary/possession aspect of rich/poor, I discovered that abundance was a mindset. A very healthy way to look at life is that I believe abundance is having more than what is needed in order that you can give to others.

Mindset will be the topic for next week, but I will raise one question here as the thought to ponder.

> **Thought to ponder**
>
> If it is true that you are only as old as you feel, can it be also true that you are only as rich or poor as you believe? Reflect on what it looks like to live an abundant life.

Day 21

TIME TO GO DEEPER
JOURNAL ACTIVITY

"But seek first the kingdom of God and his righteousness, and all these things will be added to you." Matthew 6:33 (ESV)

This week we looked at a few of the more common contrasts or as they are sometimes thought of – opposites in life. When it comes down to it though, comparing is often a trap we fall into that does not serve us well.

For the sake of this chapter, your journaling exercise is to ponder and to write what comes to mind on the various contrasts used here, as well as noting others that may come up for you.

How do you decide if someone is good vs bad? Is it the activities of life that make us categorize them in this way? How do you use these contrasts when referring to your abilities and/or short comings?

Was there a time when you did not struggle to see your beauty or allow it to shine? Have there been changes in your own viewing of yourself? Have you read the story of the ugly duckling?

What does it mean to live abundantly and what would that mindset look like for you to recognize that you are already there?

> **Read – Reflect – Pray**
>
> Psalm 81:10; Matthew 6; Luke 15; John 10

Week 4

MINDSET

*"Do not be conformed to this world,
but be transformed by the renewal of your mind,
that by testing you may discern what is the will of God,
what is good an acceptable and perfect"*
Romans 12:2 (ESV)

Day 22

IT'S ALL IN MY HEAD

"It's all in me head" says Mr. Sweeney in the movie *"Chicken Run"*. His wife reads about getting rich by making pies. When the chickens learn about this, they get organized and try to escape. It is a great movie. Often you find Mr. Sweeney seeing what the chickens are doing, but then not believing what he sees, so he says, "It's all in me head. It's all in me head."

This week I want to look at 'mindset' and how it affects the 'spark' of our inner beauty.

The power of the mind is not something new. There are many studies that talk about how powerful our thinking is and how it affects our life direction. And in the case of these 90 days, our mind can either ignite the fire within us, or it can snuff it out.

This is likely not the first time you are reading about mindset, but it is I believe truly one of the main keys that is necessary to unlocking your inner beauty.

It is outside the scope of this book to go deep into the power of the mind. There are other books that I will suggest later if you want to examine that or the various studies that focus on the various parts of the brain itself. Suffice it to say that there is indeed power in our thoughts.

> **Thought to ponder**
>
> How have you noticed your thinking affects how you see yourself? How have the thoughts you hold shape the beauty of who you are?

Day 23

MIND OVER MATTER
_____

Webster Dictionary says: "mind over matter – used to describe a situation in which someone is able to control a physical condition, problem, etc., by using the mind."

Are you a collector of sayings that help propel you forward? For me, some are quotes from my mother and others are from relatives. Some are scripture passages. When I repeat them, I feel the strength to move forward. I feel strong in who I am.

There are a great number of studies that are done on the various parts of the brain. The idea of retraining and mindset are popular topics. From my own study, I concur that your beliefs about yourself or a situation can have a direct impact on how you deal with those situations.

Consider these as some of the more popular sayings:

> "It is mind over matter. If you don't mind,
> then it doesn't matter."

> "Your mind will answer most questions
> if you learn to relax and wait for answers."

> "When the going gets tough, the tough get going."

And my newest favorite saying is from a movie, "It will all work out in the end. If it is not working out, then this is not the end."

> **Thought to ponder**
>
> What sayings do you have that help you to push forward when you feel you can't go on? Take a moment to find a few quotes and a few verses that speak to you.

Day 24

I THINK I CAN!!

In 2014, I did some major challenges that required strength, but more so it was about my mindset. One significant challenge was to participate in a 2-day bike ride to raise funds and awareness for cancer research and programs.

As I would look at a hill that was ahead, I had to do a LOT of mind work. I had trained. I had come this far. I could do it. I would often stop and look and just think of those who were fighting cancer or who had fought or who had 'lost' the fight. What was a hill in comparison?

It was others also around me – many I had never met before – who as they passed, gave me cheers to keep going. And those words of encouragement kept playing over and over.

I often thought of the childhood story of the Little Engine who climbed a mountain. He was pulling a load bigger than really the Little Engine was capable of just by saying the words over and over, "I think I can! I think I can!"

There are many verses that are written which can help us to have strength in times when we need to persevere through something.

> "If God be for us, who can be against us?"
> (Romans 8:31) ESV)

"I am able to do all things through him who strengthens me" Philippians 4:13 (CSB)

> ### Thought to ponder
>
> When you look at yourself, do you feel like you are a conqueror or that you are being conquered? What are some steps to take to be able to quote the above verses with confidence?

Day 25

PLAY IT AGAIN SAM!
___

*D*o you have a favorite movie, or song, that you like to watch/listen to repeatedly?

If I need an emotional lift, I often listen to music. There are those songs that no matter how dark the day is or how stressed I am, just listening to them brings the healing tears and the peace that comes during a storm.

Musicals are something I love to watch as well. I am thankful that early in our marriage my husband realized just how much I loved them. Often then, instead of watching Star Trek or Marvel movies, he would make a date night for us to go to a nearby dinner theater. During the times we were unable to do this, he would find a musical on TV that we both enjoyed.

There are 'tapes' that play in my mind though that don't bring this joy and peace. These are the ones that got recorded some time in the past and sometimes they play over and over again. They are tapes that spell 'defeat'. These tapes come up unknowingly and they bring with them attacks on my self-worth and my self-image.

More recently, I have become aware of one phrase that pops up as fast as a pop tart. If I did not get a job I applied for, I determined that I was not good enough. Or if I auditioned to sing and was not accepted, the same recording came up. It is a daily battle really.

Along with that are ones that say, "You are not worth the effort," or "You might as well quit now."

It is hard to fight these thoughts. It sometimes takes too much energy and the thoughts 'win' the battle. If that is the case, I might find it more difficult to find that beauty that was there shining brightly for the world to see.

A quick read through the Psalms and you can be comforted to know these emotional and psychological swings were also felt by the Psalmist. Days of victory but also days of despair.

Some days I wish I was like my computer where I could erase the negative self-talk that happens. What I realize though is that "The steadfast love of the Lord never ceases, his mercies never come to an end; they are new every morning; great is your faithfulness" (Lamentations 3:22-23) (ESV). That's the hope that moves me forward.

> **Thought to ponder**
>
> What are some inspirational things that you can do? Have you read 'The Little Engine that Could'? How does that apply to the challenges in your life today?

Day 26

DO YOU REMEMBER??

---

*I*n this theme of mindset, it is important to talk a little more about triggers. Most people are aware that we have them, but a lot of us don't really understand what is happening – it just happens.

You don't even have to be in the experience for me to trigger something for you if it is an experience that you have already had. Let me try your senses and triggers when I say these next few sentences:

> *The bread is just finished in the oven, and I have placed it to cool before cutting and putting some butter on it.*
>
> *The choir sang the Hallelujah chorus to a standing ovation.*
>
> *The rain on the tin roof of the cabin was so loud we could not hear each other speak.*
>
> *The neighbor had family over for a BBQ.*
>
> *My baby laughed at me playing Peek-a-Boo.*

Did you sense something even reading these? As simple as it is, those are triggers. They are touching a memory and for the ones listed, most of them are good memories. But some triggers bring up other emotions and thoughts and the tapes we talked about yesterday start to play again.

What about these:

> *"You will never succeed."*

> *"You are fat. skinny. ugly. stupid."*

The list can go on longer. And this is what I want you to learn: memories of experiences can trigger emotional responses, both positive ones and negative ones. But memories are not 'real' in time. They are a footprint of a past event that has been stored. And for the most part they are not the truth of who you really are….an amazing child of God as seen in Psalm 139.

Rather than "play it again" consider changing the 'script' of a perhaps painful memory. There will be time to talk more on this at the end of the week.

Thought to ponder

What are some of the past experiences you have had that trigger your emotions? What does God say about our past? Find two verses to help.

Day 27

IF ONLY

A scripture verse that I have struggled to fully understand is when Paul says that "whatever state I am in, there I am content." It aligns with the embroidered pillowcases that say things like "bloom where you are planted".

Some days I feel like I am my worst enemy because I hear myself saying "If only…" and it trips me up in my desire to be the woman I believe God has designed for me to be.

> *If only I had thought of that beforehand, things would have been better.*
>
> *If only I had kept my mouth shut, I would not have caused her to be hurt.*
>
> *If only I had listened to my mother.*

What, wait, where did that last one come from? My mother?

Yes, my mother seemed to say things and I would challenge them with "Oh Mom, you don't understand." The same could be said of my mother-in-law, but I battled her a little more with "You don't really know me."

In both situations, I was not as 'right' as I hoped to be. I felt confident in my own knowledge. Even to the point of wanting to say, "I will do it this way and show them I know what I am doing."

Except there were many times I had to return to them and say, "How did you know?"

If only – it is a defeated position and one that is also dangerous, because it is asking to be allowed to turn back time. It is the voice of regret. And it most certainly does not spark inner beauty. It may lead to it though if there are repentant tears and acknowledgement of wrong.

As of late, the words of "if only" seems to join the other thoughts of "is it too late?" What if all that I am now learning here six decades later is too late to make a difference?

I had to work through that belief statement and recognize that I still have time to be all that I am meant to be. To be all that God created me to be. I may have fallen short but that is up until this moment. With my new knowledge and humility, I can move forward. Someone has suggested having fill in the blank statements that start with either "Next time I will ____" or even "Up until now ____" to help with making the mental shift.

> **Thought to ponder**
> What are the "if only" statements in your life that might be holding you back now from being all you can be?

Day 28

TIME TO GO DEEPER
JOURNAL ACTIVITY

Jesus said, "If you have faith like a grain of mustard seed, you can say to this mountain, move from here to there and it will move. Nothing will be impossible for you."
Matthew 17:20 (ESV)

Congratulations on completing the first month of looking at ways to "Spark Your Beauty".

This week we went a little deeper into mindset. There are so many books out there on the power of the mind.

The fact remains that you are who you say you are. And with that then you have the power and ability to change – yes even your own views of yourself. There will be resistance. But the fact that you are still reading this book shows that you have a desire to be 'more', and that what you feel may still be hidden inside of you.

Did you discover some 'tapes' that continue to play? Perhaps some play even unconsciously until you realize a feeling of increased sadness or even shame. What about the triggers? Take time to reflect and then journal about the things that can trigger emotional responses within you.

What holds us back from what we want in life? To whom do we give this responsibility or blame? These are the thoughts to ponder and journal on today.

In the coming weeks we will now move on to the exterior aspects of life and how they affect our self-image and are reflected in how we evaluate our own self-worth.

Read – Reflect – Pray

Luke 12:7; Hebrews 4:16; 2 Timothy 1:7

Week 5

INTERLUDE

Day 29

UNCOMMON COMMONS

---

*I*n a few weeks we are going to go deeper about the various aspects of self (identity, image, esteem, etc.) But I wanted to take a little interlude after our first month of so much introspection to share a little more about my personal journey. To give you a little historical background if you will.

If you ever have joined a new group or gone to a gathering, the most common opening of conversation is centered around questions like "Tell us who you are, where you are from, and a little bit about yourself".

While I can answer the first question by stating my name, the two questions that follow cause me to pause. To say that I have moved a lot in my life is a bit of an understatement.

I was born in London, Ontario but we lived on the air base Alymer as my father was the Canadian Air Force Chaplain. At age 2 we moved to Bagotville, Quebec. Then at age 7 we moved to the base in Summerside, Prince Edward Island. A year later we moved into the town of Summerside. At the age of 11, we moved just outside of the city of Charlottetown to a rural area known as South Milton. We stayed there for over 4 ½ years. (My father died suddenly when I was 10).

There was more moving but basically all within the Charlottetown area until I went off to Bible College and then my first job in Halifax, Nova Scotia. When friends of mine were moving out west, my mother suggested it was a great time for me to go and travel and see the world. I did, and found myself not only living in Calgary, Alberta, but meeting and marrying my husband. Since his family all lived in and around the Calgary area, we mostly considered this 'home'. We kept moving though, sometimes for his schooling and sometimes for me for a nursing job and sometimes it was about both.

In summary then, I have lived in 9 of the 10 provinces in Canada. Outside of Canada, we have lived in Illinois, Texas, Papua New Guinea, and Tanzania. At this stage of life, Calgary is my adult home. I married here. Our sons met and married their wives here. All five of my grandchildren were born here.

So, the uncommon common for me is that it depends to whom I am speaking as to how I answer the question "where are you from". Depending on the situation I am in when asked, I often answer, "I may not know where I am from, but I know where I am going!"

> **Thought to ponder**
>
> What do you feel is the importance of knowing where you are from in how it relates to your thoughts, dreams and desires? What does it mean to you to be a 'citizen of heaven' (Philippians 3:20-21).

Day 30

WHO AM I?

Growing up I knew I was a MacKay, and I knew what the heritage and expectations were that came with that name. My father's family often came together on a regular basis, so I knew my relatives quite well.

I moved 3,000 miles away from home at the age of 21. It was a new time of people not understanding the importance of me being a MacKay. I felt a little lost. I quickly found a church home and that helped me fully understand the concept of "the family of God". I became a regular soloist at church and then worked with the children's ministry.

Just shy of my 26th birthday, I married my best friend and became Mrs. Weatherhead. Now I was no longer the MacKay person and again felt a little lost. We moved and I did not sing as often and the church we attended did not have the children's ministry.

One of my lifetime goals in life was to become a nurse and when that happened in 1987, that is how I then identified myself. One of my greatest joys was hearing Eric (my son) say "mama". More recently though, my favorite identity is being "Nana" to my grandchildren.

Living away, with my mother's failing memory, I remember the first time going to visit that she did not recognize me. My sister would say my name and there seemed to be some recognition of Jill – just she did not see me. There was a time that she did not even seem to remember "Jill", so I told her I loved her and that I now was a grandmother. I was telling a story and was quite demonstrative with my hands when she suddenly looked right at me and said, "I know you!" I treasure that moment of recognition as that was the last time that I saw her alive.

> **Thought to ponder**
>
> If you are asked "Who are you?", what is your first answer to the question? (Don't go too deep. Just take note of your first thought.)

Day 31

WHAT MAKES ME, ME?

Watching the snowflakes the other day, I was reminded how there are no two snowflakes that are identical. That is the same with us. There is only one you. There is only one me.

I grew up knowing that I resembled my mother. So much so, that when I would go back home to Prince Edward Island to visit her in a nursing home, the nurses would say right away "You are Joyce's daughter aren't you?" There may be some characteristics and facial resemblances, but it has taken a very long time for me to realize that while I may look like her, I am still unique. I am in fact me.

There have been times in my life that the 'me' has been lost. I have been unclear of expectations of others and often made mistakes from just not understanding the 'rules'. My mother went years with an undiagnosed mental illness (which we do not share) and so I often tried to change who I was to make her happy. This set up a pattern of behavior that followed me into adult life and even more so as we moved so frequently.

There have been moments in my life that I have felt like I will never measure up. I will never succeed in making everyone love me and making everyone happy.

In working on some personal development for my new business, I started reading books and it was through some of that reading and the help of coaches that I learned it is not my role in life to make everyone happy. What a freeing thought! It is also an unrealistic expectation to think that everyone will love me.

You may be at a different place in your journey, but on January 1, 2022, I declared to God that this was my year to step up and step into the woman I believed He created me to be. Writing this book is one of the first steps.

> **Thought to ponder**
>
> Have there been times or places in your life when you have felt the real 'you' was lost? What steps could you take so that the real you always shows up?

Day 32

WHO DO YOU SAY *I AM*?

I had the pleasure of spending time with three of my granddaughters a while back. Pretending to be someone else is a very common aspect of their day. Their imaginations are amazing.

The eldest was dressed as a princess, a younger version of Elsa. The middle of the three I thought was a ballerina, so she quickly made sounds to let me know that she was a monkey. When I guessed it correctly, she said, "I'm a monkey ballerina." The youngest one was not to be left behind (she was 2 at the time) and when I asked her, I laughed at her response. "I cute!" and she flashed her smile.

And this is where it all begins really. Can you think back to when you were younger? I mean go back as far as you can and see what comes up. For some of you, it may only be a short way back and for others it may be a harder exercise.

Take some time to think of all the ways people have described you. I alluded to this a few days ago when I talked about various titles that help me to define myself. Some call me a nurse. Others call me a wife, mother, sister, Nana. And there are even those who call me 'friend'.

It is not uncommon to give nick names, especially when we are children. Not all of them are flattering but mostly they are names given to describe how we are seen by the person giving the name. I prefer the names in the paragraph above to the ones that were more hurtful – slow poke, fatty, troll face, freak.

For each of these there is an aspect of the perception someone else has of you that, depending on who they are to you, may influence even your own self perception and image.

> **Thought to ponder**
>
> What is the earlier memory you have of a time someone gave you a 'nick name'? What is one unkind label you have been given? Find a scripture verse that shows the Truth about who you are.

Day 33

WHO DO *YOU* SAY I AM?
_____

Yes, the question requires a repeat. It is a question that comes up in the Bible quite a few times.

Those closest to Jesus could not understand who He was and so they kept asking him, "Who are you?" Jesus was not the first person to be asked that. His cousin John the Baptist was also asked, "Who are you?" Likewise also Paul the apostle.

You see this is a common question. It is not always worded this way. Sometimes it is said with disdain like, "Who do you think you are?" or surprise "Who is that person?"

I like the answer Jesus gave, but it was a 'test' question to see if they had been paying attention to who he really was. He said, "Who do you say that I am?"

So many times we put labels on people that don't actually fit them. And it is no surprise that most labels we put on ourselves. And this is how we determine our self-identity.

For over three decades, I have been a nurse and I'm about to retire. There is a sadness in this change because I identify as a nurse. Someone recently said that I am not my skills but in fact I *do* the skills. If that follows, then there is no 'fear' of me or how I view my identity being lost by stopping the work of actively nursing as a profession. I will still very much be me.

Who am I?

> * I am a light in the darkness, and it is a light that needs to shine.

Thought to ponder

When we think of how others see us, how related is it to our vocations? What are some of your traits that are *you* – aside from what you do?

(Matthew 16 in the Bible is where you can find how Jesus met with this question of "Who do you say that I am?")

Day 34

THE REAL YOU?

I was asked recently to describe the 'real' me. It was hard at first but with some prompting I could at least say that the real me is approachable if you need help.

I am that woman in the grocery store that you can approach and ask for help. Or if you are lost you can stop and ask me for directions. I am the person that you can call on if you need something and I will try to help. One person described me as one who had a kind enough face it makes me approachable.

The other side of this is that often I don't know the answer, but I will take the time to help you find someone who does.

I rarely think of people as strangers – they are just new friends that don't know yet they will be part of my life.

The times I shine the most are when I am serving others. I know I am blessed to be a blessing.

The project of this book is me sharing as wide and broad as I can throughout the world with the hope it will awaken the sleeping beauties.

It is those moments when you just know – know – that you are your authentic self. And it feels amazingly more powerful than anything.

And you just want to stop the world for a few moments and revel in the strength and power you are feeling.

I want to get to a place where more days are like that: those where I start off with my head high and confidence is oozing out and my light is fully shining for the world to see.

> **Thought to ponder**
>
> Do you know the moments when you are the real authentic you? Have you noticed the group of people you are with when you either 'hide' or 'shine'? List three people you know with whom you can be your authentic self.

Day 35

SUMMARY

"We all, with unveiled faces, are looking as in a mirror at the glory of the Lord and are being transformed into the same image from glory to glory; this is from the Lord who is the Spirit." 2 Corinthians 3:18 (CSB)

The purpose of this week has been to go deeper into all the ways you see yourself. This also includes all the ways you think others see you.

If you need to turn back in time to some memories, please be sure to not get stuck there. I mentioned previously that some of the journey in this book may bring up memories that are painful and/or confusing and so please reach out to someone nearby if that happens.

But the past is the past. If someone called me fatty or slow poke and it affects how I see myself today, I have the power to change that belief. I might be overweight, and I might even be slowing down with age, however the painful part of those memories is the reality of the variety of people that are in our world.

If you don't really know how to describe your own strengths, if you do not have a belief or knowledge of who is the authentic you, then be sure to find someone to help you. A few years ago as part of network marketing people would post questions like "when we first met what was your first impression of me?" or "how would you describe me to another person".

As I type this, I continue to pray for you on your journey. I want to look at some other influences that play into our belief systems especially as we learn to see ourselves for who we are.

> **Read – Reflect – Pray**
> Matthew 16; Ephesians 2:10; 1 Peter 2:9

Week 6

CULTURE AND BEAUTY

*"There is neither Jew nor Greek,
there is neither slave nor free, there is no male
and female, for you are all one in Christ Jesus."
Galatians 3:28 (ESV)*

Day 36

WE ARE ALL THE SAME?

This week I want us to look at a few cultures that exist and how they may or may not relate to how we see ourselves. Galatians tells us that we are all 'one', but I do not believe that we are to equate that with all being the same. Rather, it is a statement of unity, equality because of Christ.

As I mentioned, I spent a lot of time of my youth in Prince Edward Island (PEI). One of the views they hold is in relation to where a person is from – you either are an Islander, or you are from away. While I was not born in PEI, but because my father was (and so were my three siblings), and I can show my roots going back the four generations to the first MacKay who came over from Scotland, then I am accepted by Islanders. However, there are some who will not consider me a *true* Islander. The fact that I moved away is even misunderstood by some. Why would anyone want to live anywhere else? I have to say I have been forgiven because I married a man from the West. It is understood then that I would settle with him.

Culture is a way that we evaluate someone else's beliefs from our own worldview and belief system. A true ethnocentric person will actually go as far as to believe there is only his/her way of doing something. And in a negative way, may even go so far as to judge the other person due to the belief that his/her 'way' is in fact superior.

Let me use an easy example for you before we go deeper this week.

Up until the global event which began in March 2020, the most common greeting in Canada was a handshake. It was the pandemic that changed people's views on any kind of body contact between two people when greeting. The belief then was it would be an offense to not shake hands as a sign of respect. But not all cultures greet in this manner. Consider the cultures where it is a kiss on one or both cheeks as the way to show a respectful greeting. Or even those cultures who do not touch but bow in a state of reverence and humility.

While we might not come to an agreement on what we believe, it is interesting to note that even attempting to define cultural beliefs is not always easy. In fact, a quick Google search will show that there are various definitions. Apparently the most common thread is that when using the word 'culture' it is referring to a group of behaviours, beliefs, values, and ideas that are shared.

In this week ahead I want to look at some broader types of culture that I believe affect how we see ourselves and how we relate to others. Some of these may have more influence on your beauty than others.

> **Thought to ponder**
>
> Are there cultural beliefs that you hold when you consider the ideas surrounding beauty? List three ways your culture defines beauty as it pertains to womanhood.

Day 37

FASHION CULTURE

The fashion culture is one of the cultures I wanted to reflect on as we work to spark our inner beauty.

Initially, I did not want to share my views on this subject because I really don't understand it well enough. I do not feel that I have fashion knowledge either. I rarely shop unless I am forced to by necessity. Until recently, my favorite stores were second hand stores and Wal-Mart. Becoming part of a new community of women has caused me to look differently at the clothing and other accessories I wear in a given situation.

But fashion can be so much more than just the clothing we choose to wear. It is also expressed in other aspects of our style. In my age group, the big decision tends to be about whether to continue coloring the grey in our hair vs letting it go to have the natural changes happen. I will admit I was okay with grey hair but now that it is going white, I am struggling a bit. I have been working on a phrase that initially was "grey is the new blonde". However I prefer a stronger statement of "Silver is the new Gold".

Our self-image, self-worth, and self-esteem can all be changed just by the fashion we choose for ourselves. I remember my mother saying that she did not feel fully 'dressed' unless she was wearing lipstick. For her this was the final touch to her created look.

We certainly dress for the occasion and for the moods we are experiencing. Consider the person who declares it to be a Pajama kind of day. Even hearing that, one can picture someone who is choosing to lounge for the day. And don't get me started about shoes or we will be here for days. Suffice to say that I feel like a different person with the different shoes I am wearing.

The fashion culture can help us to feel a welcome part of society, or it can do the reverse if we feel we do not measure up to the standards.

> **Thought to ponder**
>
> What does 'fashionable' mean to you? Are you considered up-to-date on the latest trends? Are garments important to God? Have a read of Exodus 28 and take note of what you learn.

Day 38

AND A ONE AND A TWO...
FITNESS CULTURE

The fitness culture is another culture that can impact the various ways we see ourselves, especially when it comes to the topic surrounding beauty. The fitness culture that I'm thinking of specifically is physical fitness.

I have not been a fitness guru. There have been periods of my life that I have been part of an exercise type of class. Most of the time the goal seemed to be more about weight loss than necessarily becoming fit.

The overall idea of fitness does lead to improving our health. When we are at our best physically, whatever that is, we usually have less physical and mental health struggles. How we feel about our self image can have a direct impact on our feeling or believing in our beauty.

Being physically fit may seem to be mostly about the physical nature of our body. But if you google benefits to a personalized fitness program, you will be amazed that it involves going deeper than just the surface level that we can see.

The fitness culture then often dictates to us what we 'should' be doing, how often, where, and when. Do we have our own equipment in our basement so that we can work out when it suits our schedule? What is the latest equipment that will give the best overall benefit? And since we are looking at our overbooked schedule, we also want quick results in less time.

And let's join in the fashion trends that go along with the fitness culture. From the headband, or fit bit, or the shoes, there is an understanding on what is acceptable.

> **Thought to ponder**
>
> What thoughts come up as I write my thoughts about fitness? We know our bodies are the temple – how far do we need to go to honor the temple and yet not become obsessed with our physical appearance?

Day 39

WELLNESS CULTURE

---

*H*ow are you today? Because this is a very large topic, I want you to understand that I am speaking generally to this very broad topic of wellness. I will be separating the 'diet culture' to its own day later this week.

It is possible that this is more of an industry than a specific culture depending on how you evaluate the practices that you follow to maintain overall health. And that in turn means you need to know what your definition is of 'health'. For most of us, optimal lifestyle is a desire. It is more than just being 'non sick', we want to be thriving in life.

The industry may have made it more unclear. Do we need to take food supplements or just be sure we have a balanced diet? How important are regular check-ups for eyes, teeth, and overall body? How does this equate with our desire to not only live the best life possible but to extend it as far into the future as we can?

Wellness products are ones that are created to decrease stress, help with sleep, provide extra energy, heal the gut, etc. They are "anti aging, vegan friendly, toxic free." But wellness is also about taking breaks – mentally, physically, and spiritually.

If then wellness is equated with thriving, how do we measure the cost and benefits of what our present culture may dictate? Along with this, how do we find a balance to have overall health, when for many of us our lives are filled with things to do and places to be?

God took a day off after creating the world. Jesus went away from the crowds to be alone with God. Perhaps even these two examples can be our example and guide us in our wellness journey.

Thought to ponder

If God and Jesus needed time to 'regroup', what does that tell us about our need to implement this in our lives? List two more examples of ways to begin implementing "wellness" practices into your life.

Day 40

FAMILY CULTURE

───────────

This is the culture that tends to have the most influence on our belief systems. Our family of origin was the initial place where we learned the ways that are more acceptable to the group we live among.

There are other influences in this culture such as our definition of family and your position in the family (if there are other children). In a course I took in Nursing on the changes to family, even the definition of 'family' has changed in our society. Consider too the definitions between cultures.

In Papua New Guinea for example, multiple wives were considered a norm in the more rural areas of the country. When we first lived there, one of our initial tasks was to create a chart of the genealogies of the families that lived in our village. The first question of "who are your parents" brought about a discussion that went on for many months. This group of people had a variety of ways to define what I had started out thinking of as a basic question.

Regardless of our definition of family and/or its structure, it is not surprising that it is in the early years that seeds are planted and have the biggest influence on our belief system. Our family of origin then often has the biggest influence on our beliefs. These are expanded upon from where we lived growing up, where we went to school and how we see ourselves within this group of people we identify with as 'family'.

> **Thought to ponder**
>
> As you look at your own family culture, what are some things you want to retain for generations after you? Consider the importance of genealogy and family legacy found in the Scriptures. What is the relevance of the long lists found in Matthew and Luke?

Day 41

DIET CULTURE

$\mathcal{T}$oday the focus will be on the 'diet culture'. This is the one that has had the most affect on my personal wellbeing. And not in a good way.

It is rare to find someone these days who is not on a diet or if they are not on one, they are looking for the next best way to lose weight.

Now there is a shift, and many people seem to take a 'diet' simply to get a jump start. But a lot of people are recognizing that there are beliefs and mindset work that will also need to be done.

In fact, Google will show you that there is a plethora of books, courses, and coaches whose main viewpoint is the idea that diets don't work. And in fact, they are not only harmful for the most part being unbalanced in a complete nutrition sense, but they are also so restrictive that a significant number of people harm their own self-images/self-identity in the process.

Honestly, I think I have been through almost all the diets out there. There are some I've tried that did give me results, but the restrictions were too hard to maintain. And it seemed like it was more of a punishment to say, "No you are not allowed to eat that." But I also struggled with my inability to follow through with a training/course/program. I dealt with a lot of guilt for not being able to get the promised results and even had trainers tell me that I must be doing things 'wrong'.

Now the purpose of this book is not to go deeper into this topic except to say that if you are struggling with your 'size' or if you have someone saying you need to change your 'size', then be sure to do it with love and kindness. No shame. No guilt.

> **Thought to ponder**
>
> What has been your experience with the diet culture? What are some ways to accept your body the way you are, right in this moment? What do you think is the underlying misbelief in the relationship between beauty and body size?

Day 42

TIME TO GO DEEPER
JOURNAL ACTIVITY

"For the body does not consist of one member but of many... But God has so composed the body, giving greater honor to the part that lacked it, that there may be no division in the body, but that the members may have the same care for one another." 1 Corinthians 12:14, 24b-25 (ESV)

Some of the cultures talked about this week are what we can also call 'trends. It is sometimes hard to even keep up on what are the latest and greatest ideas that are happening.

Am I a person of fashion? Do I watch for the newest exercise or weight loss program? What beliefs were given to me as a child growing up that I still hold that may not be serving me well?

Do you have some clothing that you put on that makes you feel more beautiful? What says 'more' about you - the clothes you wear outside the house? or the clothes you wear when you are just hanging out at home?

As you look at the culture of your early years, let's say from birth to when you left home, do you see some of the family of origin beliefs that you continue to believe? or after you left home did you shed those and adapt to other beliefs?

Read – Reflect – Pray

Psalm 139; Galatians 3:8; 1 Corinthians 11: 1-2

Week 7

WHO INFLUENCES YOU?

"But Peter and the apostles answered, We must obey God rather than men."
Act 5:29 (ESV)

Day 43

INFLUENCES FROM OTHERS: FICTIONAL OR REAL

"For now we see only a reflection as in a mirror, but then face to face. Now I know in part, but then I will know fully, as I am fully known." 1 Corinthians 13:12 (CSB)

After a week of examining various cultures that affect how we see ourselves and the beliefs we hold, I want to talk about some specific influences on our points of view. The verse I chose for this week is about a mirror. As we move through the stages of life, things become clearer. For example, there are things that I felt my mother did wrong. When she came to help me when my last child was born, I told her that the longer I was a mother, the easier it was to forgive her. The reality is that she did the best she could with the resources she had at that time.

This week I want to look at the people (real or fictional) that have had an impact on me. The list is a lot longer than what I am sharing but I wanted to give a few examples of how these influences in our lives can help to build us up or tear us down. Some of the influences have been for good, helping me to be the woman God intended. However, the influences did not always bring about a healthy view of self.

This week will be a lot of my reflection and I hope that it will spur within you some thoughts you have about the people around you that influence you in your thinking when you look at yourself. For better or for worse.

I have gone far back in my thinking to look at some of the women that were of such influence that even now, all these years later, their words and actions toward me has a direct impact on how I see beauty in myself and in the world.

I will say that I was blessed as a child growing up to have several aunts who truly looked out for me, and as an adult I can see most of their actions were to that end.

> **Thought to ponder**
>
> What influences have you had in your life to this point that have strongly impacted how you see yourself? Make a note of these in your journal.

Day 44

A HEROINE FROM A BOOK - ANNE OF GREEN GABLES

While growing up, I loved the story of Anne of Green Gables. And she fits here as we talk about the struggles of our self image and looking to find beauty. If you have not read this story, you are really missing out. It is one of those stories that you can read at any age. I spent many of my growing up years in Prince Edward Island and I can tell you that after moving away, it was hard to read and/or watch the movies. It made me too homesick and still does. Some of the characters closely resemble some of my relatives.

How we feel about our appearance, I believe, does have an impact on our self esteem. Especially if we are also taught that beauty is about our exterior characteristics. Think of the statement that 'blondes have more fun' and how it creates a desire for those who do not share that hair color to try to determine if there is truth in the saying by coloring their hair.

Anne struggled with her appearance. It is possible partly due to other events in her life and the way people responded to her red hair and freckles. But in your early years when you are told something about how you look, it can affect you for better or worse. And spoiler alert: if you have not yet read the book, she does try to color her hair and it does not go well for her.

I want to be clear that I do not have any judgement towards the person who wants to have a specific color of hair. I am about to embark on a new campaign though that will stand up to the old "blondes have more fun" and that is to say, "Silver is the new Gold!" as I embrace the natural color shift of my hair as part of the aging process.

Thought to ponder

Is there a fictional story you grew up with in which you found yourself identifying with the main character? If not, was there a character you would like to be more like? Who was it and what did you love about them?

Day 45

DO YOU HAVE A DISNEY STORY FAVORITE PRINCESS?

Another fictional character is one of my favorites of the Disney stories. I have read other versions of this story, but the general sense is similar. Cinderella and her father are very close and when he dies, her life changes drastically.

In one movie version, Ever After (1998), the scene where he dies possibly moves me so deeply as I too was close to my father who died of a heart attack when I was quite young. The similarity of our lives stops there. My mother was living, and my sister was not mean to me.

Yet the part of the Cinderella story that remains the same, even with the remakes, is that no matter what the hardship was that she faced, she was able to remain 'beautiful'. This was shown by her continued love and kindness to others no matter how she was treated in return.

In the movie in 2015, I love the twist at the ending when at the last moment before going off with her prince, Cinderella turns and faces her mother. "I forgive you" she says and then turns away.

And that is the true beauty of Cinderella. A kind and forgiving heart.

The influences of this story in how she lived her life helped during the times when I felt that beauty was more about what is on the inside than what is on the outside.

I will admit to also believing that one day someone would see my original beauty, fall in love with me and we would live 'happily every after'. This is not a topic of being single or married. It is to just explain one of the influences in my life that shaped some beliefs specifically on how it pertains to my definitions and understanding of 'beauty'.

Is it possible there are other lessons that we can learn from this fairy tale?

> **Thought to ponder**
>
> What are some possible lessons we can learn and apply from this fictional story? What relationship is there between the fruit of the Spirit and the way Cinderella is described? Is there a different story that has impact on how you evaluate beauty?

Day 46

HABITS THAT ARE
A RESULT OF INFLUENCES

The various cultures looked at a few days ago have the potential to influence how we see ourselves. Some of these cultures will even bring about some habits that will either help to build up our confidence or have the opposite affect.

If we are trying to make a fashion statement, then we look to the media to help us to know what to wear to make that statement. The shifts in fashion could have us puzzled on what is expected when we attend various functions.

Adopting a healthy lifestyle will mean being influenced by how that is defined. I remember when jogging was the encouraged way to get healthy. Today the emphasis is more to make a habit of having regular movement throughout your day to keep healthy.

The influences of society in general by what is on TV, or in the news, or in the latest magazines, will bring about a level of evaluation that may find us moving towards a thought of scarcity and lack. This goes along with the old idea of keeping up with the Joneses.

A generational habit also influences us. If we are taught to not speak of our accomplishments because it is seen as being vain, then we will not celebrate wins. The wrong use of humility will have the ability to create a habit and belief that we should stand with our head down in more of a state of bowing down.

The actions of our parents and the habits they lived out in front of us is another influence that will affect our views on beauty. For example, did you hear your father compliment your mother on anything? Or give a word of thank you for the meal prepared for example? This habit influences what you then expect in your home when you move away.

> **Thought to ponder**
>
> What habits do you have that help give you confidence? If struggling with confidence, what are three habits you can start to implement in your life to help with your confidence?

Day 47

WHAT DOES IT MEAN TO BE A WOMAN?

---

*I*n trying to find myself as a young girl, I felt that I did not always fit in. Playing with dolls and barbies was not quite my cup of tea. I much preferred to do more of a rumble tumble type of play. My relatives called me a tom boy because of my desire to be outside playing vs sitting quietly reading.

During my teen years, in the summer, I often helped this family without children. I thought of them as very old at the time and now I wonder if they were just barely in their 60's? Fred, Bert and Elsie had the bigger farm while Gerald lived with his wife Nellie on the T intersection of highway where I was living at the time. Often in the summer you would find me helping with bringing in the hay or just 'mucking' the barn. I loved helping with the hay. I had hay fever so bad, but still the thrill of throwing bales like the guys or driving the truck or tractor or the huge meal that was prepared for us once we were done all was so much worth it. These five adults thought of me as beautiful, and I loved the time I had with them.

Acceptance by others has a significant impact on how we see ourselves. For me it was fun to help these people and the payment of the amazing meal was more than enough as a thank you.

The changes of the roles of the woman in society have changed significantly, especially after World War II. While it goes back further to a group of women fighting to get the right for women to vote, it was in the 1960's that the women's liberation movement seemed to cause a larger fight for equality.

From my experience of living in a developing country, the women of Papua New Guinea have a long way to go when it comes to being a value in society.

There is great political debate in my province and country that discusses even the concepts of gender. It goes outside the scope and purpose of this book to talk about that subject. Suffice it to say that my point is that God creates us as individuals. And self acceptance along with acceptance of His love for us is the key to sparking the beauty He created.

Thought to ponder

Take some time to read the characteristics of Proverbs 31. Write down three you see in yourself. How does knowing this help with loving yourself for who you are?

Day 48

MY MOTHER
___

*P*erhaps the greatest influence on our beauty comes from the teachings from our mother. Or at least the matron influence as you are growing up. In fact, in some of my personal development courses recently there has been a theme mentioned of the ideas behind generational healing. It is outside the scope of this book and certainly not my expertise, but I want to mention it here because I think there is value in what is being suggested. But first let me tell a funny story to explain this idea of generational influence.

The story is told of a newlywed preparing a roast for the first time in her new home. Her husband watched her cut one inch off each side of the roast before putting it in the pan to cook. He was curious and so asked her what she was doing. "It is what my mother always did." Curious now, she called her mother to ask for the reason behind the practice. "It was what my mother did." So now the phone call was to the grandmother who answered, "I had to cut the roast to fit in the pan."

My mother's mother did not necessarily teach in a way that was helpful. There were hard times when my mother was growing up (the depression) and my mother was the youngest of five children – only two would live to be adults.

We have two ways we respond to our mother's teaching or the lack thereof. We adopt it because, well, she is our mother. Or we disagree and set with determination to be the opposite.

It was usually about my hair. Even when I would come home to visit there would be the look, if not the added comment. Fact is, she loved my hair short. Even to this day, especially if my bangs are misbehaving, I hear my mother's voice, "Your hair is in your eyes". I can remember the times she would lick her fingers first and then try to get my bangs to the left or the right. Or the mortifying times when she would grab the scissors and decide to cut them.

Even when I moved far from my childhood home, the voice in my head was still my mother and even to this day I sometimes hear her voice. It was not always a good tape that was playing. Though now that she is gone, I'd be OK to hear her voice again even if it was to correct me.

There was a lot I did not understand about the way she showed her love. To her credit, she did a lot with limited training and support. Becoming a widow at 39 could not have been easy. She also lived more than half her life with an undiagnosed mental condition. I'm thankful that I had an older sister and my aunts who also looked out for my well being when my mom could not.

Thought to ponder

What are some of the ways your relationship with your mother has shaped how you see yourself? Regardless of how this relationship was, take time reading and reflecting on Paul's thoughts towards our relationships with other women (1 Timothy 5:2).

Day 49

TIME TO GO DEEPER
JOURNAL ACTIVITY

"But by the grace of God I am what I am, and his grace toward me was not in vain. On the contrary, I worked harder than any of them, though it was not I, but the grace of God that is with me." 1 Corinthians 15:10 (CSB)

A focus of this chapter on influences is to set the stage for what we will look at next week as we go deeper to look at the various 'selfs'.

I believe our relationship with other women either creates strength within in us or it causes hurt and pain. There are those years where competition is high. Value is put on popularity.

Do you find yourself with a lot of women friends? Is this something that comes easy to you, or do you find it difficult to 'fit in'?

I recognize part of my struggle in fitting in is related to the many moves and therefore not taking the time to understand the differences between people in general.

What influences you then? Are there people in books, fictional or real? Or family members and friends that inspire you?

You chose to take this journey with me and so I am now an influence, for better or worse, as you seek to discover the inner parts of you.

Imagine if we just embraced each other for our differences. If we could accept the sisterhood and be united. Standing tall to be the leaders for those around us. Opening the floodgates from within to let our beauty and strength shine and change this world.

> **Read – Reflect – Pray**
> Proverbs 13:20; Proverbs 27:17; Titus 2

Week 8

THE VARIOUS SELFS

"Do not let your adorning be external — the braiding of hair and the putting on of gold jewelry, or the clothing you wear — but let your adorning be the hidden person of the heart with the imperishable beauty of a gentle and quiet spirit, which in God's sight is very precious."
1 Peter 3:3-4 (ESV)

Day 50

WHAT SELF IS IT THAT IS YOU?

The way we look and see ourselves is key to how we show up in the world today. Not how we show up to others, but how we show up for ourselves.

Prior to this writing project, I had focused on learning about self-esteem, self-image, and self-care. I read a lot of information to find out what these really mean and how factors in our lives help or determine the growth in certain aspects of 'self'.

One conclusion for me was that there is actually a list of 'selfs' and I am going to focus on five of the more common ones: self-image, self-esteem, self-worth, self-concept, and ideal self.

In the interlude a few weeks ago, I shared my story as I sought to determine who I am and that in turn has helped me to discern who I am meant to be. There are various lists and titles that define who I am. Labels I have put on myself related to relationships, vocations, hobbies.

Who am I?

>I am a sister, wife, mother, mother-in-law, grandmother.
>
>I am a nurse, a writer, a singer, a comedian.
>
>I am a cyclist, a promoter, a friend.

And perhaps most importantly, so I left it to last – I am a child of God.

Who we are or who we think we are or who we would like to be – these all factor into this idea of "what is beauty - where do I find it - how do I spark it - how do I keep it alive?"

Thought to ponder

How would you describe yourself?

Day 51

WHAT IS MY IMAGE OF MY 'SELF'?

To answer the question, "Who am I?" the first rebuttal question might be: "In what context?" Part of the answer to this question is related to our self-image – that is how we see ourselves. It often involves specific characteristics (I am tall/short), personality traits (I am kind, I am a hard worker), or even social roles (I am a nurse/ I am a teacher).

Our self-image changes as we go through this journey of life, sometimes because of some of the 'battles' that occur around us. If we marry and have children, our self-image may get blurred into the additional views society and family may give us. Are these the images of who we are or are they various roles that we play?

A quick glance in a bookstore or library and you will find many books that are written to address the topic of self-esteem. I am not going to delve too deeply. That is not my training or expertise.

I do struggle with this one though, mostly because for years it was more a struggle of wanting to please others. My image of myself seemed determined by the evaluation given to me by others. It is a rather dangerous place to be, though, I am realizing now.

It is not hard to see then that understanding our self-image takes more than just a quick look in the mirror. Or a look at a photograph.

While these might be how we see ourselves, neither the photo nor the mirror gives us a true representation of who we are.

> **Thought to ponder**
>
> How would you describe your image?

Day 52

I THINK THIS, AND SO IT IS

Self-esteem is more linked with our evaluated opinion of who we are. Some people might have a high self-esteem, and in that case, we often think of that person as being arrogant and/or proud. Or we might have a low self-esteem which will have a direct impact on the way we see ourselves and how well we then travel on this journey called life.

Either extreme of self-esteem could affect this inner beauty we are so looking to find and spark.

This is more than just how I see myself. It is where the beliefs I hold are played out in moving forward with dreams and with the motivation, or lack thereof, to see the fulfilment of those dreams.

Closely related to the idea of self-image, self-esteem may have the potential to be more affected by the environment in which we find ourselves living. As we age and add various life experiences, our-self esteem may be enhanced or thwarted.

I remember hearing of someone's school experience. They were picking teams for a sport. He was not picked last. In fact, he was not picked at all as the team decided they would rather play 'short' than have him on the team.

Ouch. The self-esteem took a hit. But not just that, it also planted a seed of the thought that "I'm not good enough."

Unlike some of the other 'selfs' we are looking at this week, self-esteem is not considered fixed. It is something we have power to change.

I do feel that my self-esteem was too closely connected to my sense of worth. There are times when achievements have helped me to be okay with who I am. I struggled with learning to love myself and yet not becoming vain or bitter.

> **Thought to ponder**
>
> When it comes to self-esteem, do you feel yours is healthy? Or needs help?

Day 53

I SEE WHAT I SEE...
BUT I'D LIKE TO SEE...
_____

Ideal Self. This is the 'self' that often is our guide through life. It is the image of what we aspire to be, and in some respects, we are already there, but maybe don't believe we are?

Dreaming as a young girl, I had a list of dreams that started with "One day...". Some things were physical and some of them were more about personality traits that I wanted to possess.

My father died when I was only 10 and so for many years my main goal in life was to do him proud, even if he would never know. When I met Jesus personally as a teenager, I desired to be the woman God created me to be. I want to be the best wife and mother. I wanted to have compassion for those I care for during my nursing career. It is in the realm of self-acceptance that there are some things that I am not to change and there are some I am.

Ideally? I would like to be Wonder Woman – fighting for justice. To help the helpless. To make sure everyone feels wanted and loved and worthy. I must admit I would not mind looking like the actress that portrays her. To be strong physically. To have long flowing hair. To not be overweight. To not be petty when things don't go the way I think they should.

And then as this ideal Wonder Woman, I would help others find themselves. Those around will throw off the covers, masks, break the walls, and release their beauty into a world that so very much needs it.

> **Thought to ponder**
>
> Do you have an image of your ideal self?

Day 54

WHAT ABOUT MY WORTH

Worthy. How do we determine our 'self-worth'? In general, we evaluate our 'worth' based on our abilities and our performance in one or more activities that we deem valuable.

Fifty years ago as part of a beauty campaign, the phrase "because I'm worth it" started a change in the beauty industry. You can google to read more about the movement of L'Oreal and how they have advanced their position today to talk about similar aspects of beauty that I have been sharing – the inner, deeper, soul beauty.

For better or worse, our understanding of our self-worth has been influenced by those around us and the success or failures we faced. If we experienced unconditional love, we are more likely to have a strong sense of personal value.

Successful experiences also lead to a higher sense of self-worth.

In a previous week, I talked about the triggers and the tapes that play in our minds. "I am not good enough," is the tape that plays most in my mind and strongly affects my self-worth.

The bottom line I believe is that when it comes to self-worth, we must be gentler with the judgements we make as we do our self-evaluation. This is the biggest reason for my "SparkYrBeauty" concept. Not everyone recognizes that they have this beauty and value.

Remember the Care Bears? It would be like that – a superpower within us that is meant to shine out and have impact on this world.

> **Thought to ponder**
> How do you feel about your self-worth?

Day 55

SELF-CONFIDENCE

Have you read of the shepherd boy David? Or the story of Gideon? Have you read of how Elijah stood up to the priests and then fled for his life in the following chapters?

These stories show us a variety of confidences. To stand up or to be cowering and hide.

At one point in time, I had full confidence in my singing ability. I sang solos and during my teen years I sang duets with my sister. I met with some famous people like Amy Grant who encouraged me to just keep playing and singing. She told me that if God gave me a song, then I was to sing it. The number of people to hear it was not important.

I remember the first time I auditioned for a singing group and was not accepted. Some of my confidence slipped. I continue to sing in church. I often was invited to sing at weddings, funerals, grave sides.

At times when I struggled with my self-confidence, I realize now that it was when people were correcting me, I kept hearing the wrong message. The voices in my head said things like, "You are not good enough". It has only been in the last few years that I realize how much of my personhood I lost in trying to make everyone else happy. To be what they wanted me to be.

January 1, 2022, marks the day when I said enough is enough. It was a day that I said that I was going to be me. I would need to learn who she was in the full, but in the writing of this book, I feel I am closer to finding her.

> **Thought to ponder**
>
> What abilities or talents do you have that give you a sense of self-confidence?

Day 56

TIME TO GO DEEPER
JOURNAL ACTIVITY

How is your 'self' now?

When I started looking at ways to spark beauty, I realized that I had to start with myself. What I did not realize was how many layers it would take to find the real me.

Have you seen the movie Shrek, where he talks about ogres being like onions? That is how I have felt as I study and read about the various 'selfs' such as we have looked at this week.

Of all the selfs that we talked about this week, self-confidence is the one I am working on the most. Prompted by a coach, I made a list of things accomplished – dreams that came true.

Here is just a short list of some accomplishments, some dreams that have come true in the past 30 years (the dream list was created when my second son was born; the fulfilment of these dreams was noted on his 31st birthday):

- travel around the globe literally (more than once actually)
- move to a foreign country and live in a remote jungle (1997)
- have a solo part in a musical (2003)
- graduate with Bachelor of Nursing (2010)

- cycle over 200 km over two days for cancer research (2014 and continue this each year)
- complete a triathlon (2014 and the following 4 years)
- become Nana (I have five grandchildren now)
- go on a cruise (I've been on 3 to date)
- have a week-long vacation in a place like Mexico (now a regular every 2 years or so)

When I read this list, I can feel my body change from a slight slump to a straightening of my spine. I feel the increased confidence. And a 'knowing'. A knowing that while I still have some things left to do in my life, I have accomplished many of the dreams I desired.

Take some time to write down some of your accomplishments. Celebrate the wins of your life.

Read – Reflect – Pray
Galatians 6:4; Psalm 20:4; Acts 16:11-15

Week 9

A SEASON OF GIVING

"If you pour yourself out for the hungry and satisfy the desire of the afflicted, then shall your light rise in the darkness and your gloom be as the noonday. And the LORD will guide you continually and satisfy your desire in scorched places and make your bones strong; and you shall be like a watered garden, like a spring of water, whose waters do not fail."
Isaiah 58:10-11(ESV)

Day 57

FROM THE INSIDE OUT

This is another interlude in a sense, to all the introspection that we have done. Not all of it is easy and sometimes we need to focus on the beauty that exists by reaching outside of ourselves. So this week, I am going to give you some actual activities to do each day that will help to spread light to others.

Life is so much better and sweeter when we look outside of ourselves. This book is looking deeply at our inner self, but we need to be sure that we realize that this is not our only purpose to being here on Earth. In fact, with the same belief that I hold that we are all created beautiful, I hold the belief that we were meant for relationship with others.

Let's take a week and spend it in giving. Then like the verse in Isaiah we will not only spread love, joy, hope, and light, but in doing so it will also spark our beauty. This will bring about the promise of healing to you as well.

Thought to ponder

How does doing something for others bring light to our souls? Think of a time someone did something unexpectedly for you and what your emotional response was.

Day 58

YOU'VE GOT MAIL!!!

My sister and my mother-in-law (when she was alive) are both well known for filling mailboxes. Both seem to know everyone's special days – birthdays, anniversaries – you name it, and they have a card for it. But even outside of a special day, sometimes they would find a card and get prompted to send it with a love note inside.

Writing notes and sending cards seems to be a bit of a lost art today. And yet, I do go to the mailbox with the expectation that something will be there more than the flyers, bills, or charity requests for donations.

But like anything, if you want to see some changes in your life, you may need to start with yourself. Perhaps this is something you are already practiced at doing.

This week has two tasks for you to take time to do. I hope you will do both.

The first task I want you to do is to write yourself a note of thanks. And I want you to mail it. Why? Because the writing is the first part to acknowledge your worth but the receiving of it will be very special as well – you will see.

The second task is to mail a thank you note to someone that has been significant in your life. You can write a note or just say, "Thank you!" It is okay if you do more than one.

> **Thought to ponder**
>
> Have you received mail like this that touched your soul? How did you feel, writing to yourself? Be sure to take note of what response you have when you get the card in the mail. Maybe make a habit of doing this regularly to remind yourself that you love you!

Day 59

WHO IS CALLING?

───────────

*I*t was not that long ago that when the phone rang, the next thought would be, "I wonder who that is calling at this time of day." While I lived in the West, my sister lived in the UK, and my mother would get the time zones mixed up. Everyone in the house knew when the phone rang extra early in the morning that it was likely my mother. I never minded as it was always good to hear her voice.

I am sorry to admit that I don't use the phone like I once did. I communicate much more these days via Messenger texting to be honest. Even texting I'm not a huge fan of – but I do love to communicate and connect. Since I have lived in a myriad of places, and now that my mother and mother-in-law are gone, I find the phone is rarely used for a phone call.

As I mentioned already, I believe that we were created for relationship. And when we connect with others this also can spark our inner beauty. (And yes, I am an extrovert with a capital E!)

Your task today then is to place a phone call to someone that you don't talk to regularly. Just connect. Say hello and let them know you are thinking of them. Take a moment to pray and see what names pop up. If more than one person, write it down on your calendar to connect with those to whom you have been prompted to do a reach out towards.

Thought to ponder

How did that make you feel when they said, "Thank you for calling,"? If you got their answering machine, be sure to leave a message.

Day 60

A DAISY A DAY

There is an old song which I have enjoyed called "A Daisy a Day". (My favorite music video can be found at https://www.youtube.com/watch?v=g5AzmEX-txw). It is a beautiful love story between two people. If you have not heard it, I will give you a warning that it might move your heart in a way that a tear or two escapes.

Getting flowers from someone certainly is a way to spark beauty, don't you think?

My husband has often surprised me not only with flowers but knowing that the occasion called for the flowers he gave (such as our special anniversaries). But for today, I want to tell you about one of my son's gifts for my birthday a few years ago.

What he gave me are plastic flowers – open roses that are pink – in a lovely vase. I still see the grin on his face as he handed this gift to me. I look at them now on the center of my table and again feel the love of the gift. They are plastic, but that is part of him knowing me well. We live in a basement where flowers do not really survive.

Today then, I would like you to get some flowers and give them to someone. It can be someone special – or it can be someone you have just met. The fun of this today will be for you to determine who, when, and where.

> ### Thought to ponder
> If you like getting flowers, what stops you from buying them for yourself? Consider while you are out buying for someone else to pick up a bouquet for you!

Day 61

HOW ARE THINGS IN YOUR CORNER OF THE WORLD TODAY?

———————

Another way to spark beauty and ignite the beauty within us and others is getting together with others. Making time for this activity is not always easy but it is well worth it.

Just like having a phone call or face time visit, staying connected is a great way to boost your beauty from the inside out.

I have these two very close friends. These are women who have known me for many years. We don't see each other as often as would be nice, but when we do meet up it is like we pick up where we left off. I love when we grab a coffee together. I feel so much richer for the time spent together.

So, today your task is to make a coffee or lunch date or perhaps a walk date with someone you've been meaning to spend time with, but life has gotten in the way. If they are feeling pressured for time, agree on a time that you can at least start by penciling it in.

It would be great if this giving of your time is in person but if that is not as easy for you, then do an internet connect like FaceTime or Zoom. It may surprise you how much beauty it will spark into your day – and his/hers!

> **Thought to ponder**
>
> How does connecting with others create beauty? What does God say about fellowship with others?

Day 62

PAYING IT FORWARD

———————————

Have you seen the movie by this title? Even if not, the concept of 'paying it forward' was not new to the movie and it is not likely new to you the reader.

There was a time when we had a need. Someone gave us the money to help us with the need and at the time they said, "We do not want you to pay us back. But some time in the future, if someone presents to you a need they have, then do so and think of us."

My favorite story about receiving a gift happened during my son's cancer journey. Our budget was tight, and I struggled with unhealthy attitudes towards spending money. Close friends sent us some money in a card and the card said, "Here is some bubble gum money." I did not fully understand until reading the entire note, but the idea was that we could 'blow' the money however we saw fit. As struggling missionaries who had to keep track of how we spent money, this was such a freeing gift.

Recently, friends of mine on a similar journey were struggling and I was thrilled to be able to send them the bubble gum money. In this way, I paid it forward.

The beauty of this type of giving is that it is truly about the giving and not the receiving. Today we also have the idea of doing random acts of kindness. Doing something for someone with no expectation of receiving anything in return.

Your task today then is to pay it forward by finding a way to show a random act of kindness.

Here are just a few ideas:

- Smile and say thank you to a person serving you
- Donate used towels/blankets to animal rescue shelters (yes, they take stained ones)
- Give your spot in line to the person behind you
- Pay for coffee for someone behind you
- Shovel snow for the neighbor when you go out to do your section

> **Thought to ponder**
>
> How does it feel to do it as a random act vs doing something expected? Check out https://www.randomactsofkindness.org/the-kindness-blog for some more ideas. Take some time to get creative as you make your own list.

Day 63

TIME TO GO DEEPER
JOURNAL ACTIVITY

"Give, and it will be given to you. A good measure, pressed down, shaken together and running over, will be poured into your lap." Luke 6:38 (CSB)

We have spent many weeks so far in our journey thinking of inner beauty. This week of giving was intended to bring that beauty to the world. I believe that one of our higher callings is to show love to others.

Pulling away from all the personal development to take some time for others, you will see that this too brings not just a spark but an actual glow. We do not give in order to get a reward, but we can know there will be a blessing from God if we are doing it with a pure heart.

Kindness can go a long way these days in improving society. There is a sense of 'it's all about me'. I am part of the Baby Boomer generation and collectively we are considered the "me" generation. Some have dubbed the Millenials as the 'me me me' generation. Either way, we know that we need to have a balance. Not all about me and not all about them.

For a blog that has some great pay-it-forward suggestions: https://www.randomactsofkindness.org/the-kindness-blog.

Take some time to get creative as you make your own list.

> **Read – Reflect – Pray**
>
> Mark 9:41; Matthew 19:21; Philippians 2:4

Week 10

TIME OF CELEBRATION

"This day shall be for you a memorial day, and you shall keep it as a feast to the Lord; throughout your generations, as a statute forever, you shall keep it as a feast." Exodus 12:14 (ESV)

Day 64

TAKE TIME TO CELEBRATE

No matter when you are doing your 90 days, you are going to find some point that you will need to pause and celebrate a holiday. It might be as simple as the ones that are celebrated nationally or locally, or it might be family type of celebrations (anniversary, birthdays etc).

Family traditions and cultural practices often dictate what is expected for these special days. And herein becomes an expectation of what elements of the special day we are to have as part of the celebration.

Some childhood traditions carry forward into adulthood. Some stay behind for various reasons. Now married, I began to learn to share traditions of our family of origin and make new ones for ourselves.

We have a big calendar that has all our appointments and I circle what I call Red Letter Days. These are days that we need to think ahead and plan something special. More on that as we read on this week.

Either way, there are holidays that we look forward to celebrating and ones that may bring a sadness or even depression. If some days are harder than others when it comes to holidays, consider creating some new traditions. This week we will look at some specific holidays that are on the calendar, but I also want you to start thinking of some new ways to celebrate and create some new "red letter" days!

> ### Thought to ponder
>
> Do you have a calendar that has all the Red-Letter Days on it? Take a moment to look ahead to this month or the month ahead and see what is coming up that the calendar has marked as a special day. Pray about how to make this a Red-Letter Day in your life and the life of those around you.

Day 65

HAPPY BIRTHDAY!

You may not be a social media fan, but I have to say that I enjoy Facebook for reminding me of birthdays. It is one of the first things that I do every day – look and see whose birthday it is, and I go and wish them the best day possible. I love that on my birthday, a significant number of my Facebook friends also send me a greeting.

Not everyone celebrates their birthday. My sister started a tradition where on her birthday she went and did something special with our mother. It was her way of giving thanks to Mom for bringing her into the world.

I am not proud to say that when we got married, I felt the need to explain to my husband the importance of my birthday and what was expected. I'm ashamed to admit that I made it such a stressor for him in the early years.

It was not as easy for him, but he did become resourceful over the years. I also became less demanding. In fact, I realized that what I wanted most was for someone to sing the traditional song and to be able to have a candle to make a wish and blow it out.

There are some very significant birthday surprises that he had for me. I believe the one for my 50th still stands out as the best birthday ever. I do remember telling him that it made up for many years of forgetting and then quickly added that it did not mean it covered all forward birthdays.

The point is, I believe you should celebrate if for no other reason than that you made it another 365ish days. You are worthy of being celebrated. So, if no one is around you, go get what you need to feel celebrated. Put on something nice to wear. Got eat at your favorite food place. Or order in and enjoy a movie that brings both laughter and tears.

And this is even more important if it is one of the birthdays that we consider "Milestone" (ie 21, 30, 40, 65 etc). If these are what you consider your milestone birthdays, be sure to plan ahead. Have really big thoughts (like inviting over your five favorite people for dessert) and a few smaller ones (buy yourself a special piece of jewelry or take some time away on your own – in nature if you can).

Thought to ponder

If you celebrate birthdays, what is the one element of the day that is most important to you? What would be one thing you could do for your upcoming birthday that would help you to celebrate the day?

Day 66

VALENTINES DAY

Do you know the story that is behind this practice? I have heard a few versions, but I love that a church I attended made the month of February love month. It was more than just the 14th. It was a month to do those random acts of kindness that we talked about.

I am a bit of a romantic and so growing up I always dreamed that the man of my dreams would bring me roses, or candy, or both. Or at least a card. Have I mentioned Norm's reactions to birthdays? This one was even less well known to him. His response was something that changed our marriage (for the better) as he said "I am not into tradition. I don't want to tell you only on one day of the year that you are special and that I love you. I want to tell you every day."

Awe, is that not sweet? And I can tell you that he is quite the romantic. In our 38 years together, he still comes up with those moments of surprise. One year he arranged for a babysitter and took me to a private place, brought in food and music (on a cassette tape) and candlelight. I feel very loved in those moments because I can see that it was well thought out and planned. And now that I don't expect it, the time together is really what is most special.

Thought to ponder

What do you think of the idea of celebrating "love month" as a way to spark not just your beauty but for the person who receives your 'love'?

Day 67

ANONYMOUS ANNIVERSARY

The anniversary that I am writing about today is specific to a wedding anniversary, but it could also apply to the expectations of any day that is marked as special on the calendar. I recognize that I am married, and you might not be in the same position of life. You might be single, as in never married, or you might be dealing with the loss of your marriage partner through death or divorce. The following story still has value as an example of how important it is to tell someone close to us the significance of a day that is special to you.

Despite his lack of knowledge, reflecting back, I am surprised that my husband loved me so much that he listened and worked very hard to understand not only what dates I found important, but why they were important to me.

I want to share about our 10th anniversary because it was a turning point for both of us.

We had gone through some very hard times, and we found ourselves in counselling. My main complaint was that I felt that Norm did not value me. I used events like special dates on the calendar as my example. The counsellor made a suggestion.

I was to write in Norm's Day timer for him to order one dozen pink roses to be delivered. I did not see how that would be special since I was telling him what I wanted. What I can tell you though, is that when I opened the door and a delivery man was there holding one dozen pink roses on the day of our 10th anniversary, I cried. Even though I had put it in his day timer, I was shocked that he did it.

They were the most beautiful roses I had seen up to that point in time. They made the room beautiful, and they bloomed for weeks to come. I say, 'up to that time', because Norm has caught on now and there have been many times that he has surprised me with flowers. Each time I have to say I feel so loved and so very beautiful.

There are more anniversaries that stand out like this one shared, then the ones where life got in the way and our celebration was not exactly what I was thinking it would be like. That leads me to my main point of this chapter actually.

Sometimes our feelings of lack of worth or feelings of being unloved is because those around us do not understand the expectations we have to celebrate certain days in the year. Learning to speak up and share with someone what we want, need or desire is one step that you can take going forward.

Thought to ponder

What days on your calendar do you consider as "anniversaries"? (ie graduation from high school and/or university; moving into your first 'home'; job promotions) What activities would you like to do to celebrate and think of who you would like to have join you in your celebration?

Day 68

MOTHER'S DAY

Mother's Day I feel is one of the harder times to celebrate. If you are living and breathing, then at some point you had a mother carry you in her womb and bring you into this world.

Mother's Day might be difficult for many reasons. A friend recently sent a poem that was a Mother's Day wish to all women. It was also to those who did not even know who their mother was; or their mother was no longer living; or they did not cherish their mother. I remember a very difficult Mother's Day when I should have been holding a baby, but she had died before being born. I know there are many women who have that same pain. I have a co-worker who longed to be a mother and due to cancer, had to have a hysterectomy while she was in childbearing years. Working Maternity for the majority of my nursing career, I know of many who for reasons known or unknown are unable to have children.

Years ago, when phoning people meant the use of land lines, I had to plan to get up early to phone my mother. It was very important to her that I call her on her birthday and on Mother's Day. She said that to hear my voice on those days made her day. True story is that if I overslept (I lived 3 time zones west of her at this time), the lines were so overloaded I could not get through. And there was no other way to communicate with her. No texting. No social media. No email. I did not like myself very much on those days because I knew I had let her down. When we moved across the Pacific, she then reduced the expectation to my sending a card. There was an aspect of her belief that if I did not do these things it equated with my not loving her.

If you had a good relationship with your mother, then this day is a great day to honor her. If you did not, then perhaps you can look for the woman who has mentored you in life. We have talked about the influence of our mothers on our self image and self esteem. So, do we honor her for carrying us and delivering us into the world? We should.

I was blessed with amazing 'older women' for most of my life and an amazing Mother-in-Law who loved me unconditionally.

> **Thought to ponder**
>
> How can we find a way to celebrate the women in our lives? Who are the five most influential female mentors and what are some ways that you can celebrate them?

Day 69

CHRISTMAS

Christmas – the most wonderful time of year! The lights, the sounds, the music, the parties, the presents, and the expectations!

We are overwhelmed with what we are to buy, what we are to wear and even what food we are to eat. There is a pressure to perform. To have the perfect Christmas.

This can be a very difficult time for many. There was a difficult Christmas for me when I told Norm that there would be no Christmas that year as I stared at my flat stomach that should have been the size Mary would have had while carrying Jesus. The year when Eric my son was on cancer treatment and while we were now back in Canada, due to his being immune compromised, we also then could not celebrate it with others in the way we longed to do.

For me, the best part of Christmas are the songs and the lights. Candlelight services are the best to bring us back into the reason for this season. I still remember my first one as a child.

My father was the Air Force Chaplain and had arranged for me to be the first to walk into the service carrying a candle. My mother was afraid I would burn down the chapel, but my dad was firm with his decision.

At the appointed moment while behind me the choir sang Silent Night, I walked up the aisle towards the front. The wax dripping burnt my hands, and the fullness of the chapel made me nervous. But I saw the look on my father's face at the front of the church. He smiled with such pride and in that moment, I felt like the most beautiful person in the world.

The Hope that had come. The Light of the world. We would never again be in complete darkness. Ah yes Christmas.

> **Thought to ponder**
>
> What tradition of Christmas do you practice that brings the beauty to light? What is something new you could bring to deepen the meaning of the holiday?

Day 70

TIME TO GO DEEPER
JOURNAL ACTIVITY

"They will give a testimony of your great goodness and will joyfully sing of your righteousness." Psalm 145:7 (CSV)

There are a few main holidays that I highlighted here, but really the list could be longer. Perhaps you want to plan a family vacation. Or any vacation. Is there such a thing as a perfect vacation? A perfect holiday?

That now depends on what you think through as you journal today. What celebrations have you had in this past year that warmed your heart? What ones make you sad every year, so much that you just want to run away and hide?

May I suggest that the best ones when you journal you will see are ones that you felt loved. And you gave love. Perhaps even the ones that you had lowered your expectations of others and of yourself.

A special event in our life might mark a time that we felt the most significant and our beauty was so sparked that we could not help but shine. Or it might be that these holidays did the reverse, where they are a point of pain and disappointment. And we feel ugly as we pull away and into ourselves. Or we protect our small spark and keep it to ourselves so that no one can put out the flame with hard words or actions of neglect.

Take some time then to decide, will you find a reason to celebrate? Will you lower your expectations on what it should look like? Will you love yourself even if others do not show you the love you are longing for? Will you lift your glass of water, coffee, tea – whatever is in your cup – and say "l'chiam" – to life?

> **Read – Reflect – Pray**
> Psalm 118:1; Philippians 4:4; John 15:11

Week 11

A NEW LOOK

*"Behold, I am doing a new thing;
now it springs forth, do you not perceive it?
I will make a way in the wilderness
and rivers in the desert."
Isaiah 43:19 (ESV)*

Day 71

OUT WITH THE OLD – IN WITH THE NEW

There was a time that I remember looking out the window and informing my husband that a storm was coming. He looked out the window and disagreed. He told me that there was not even a cloud in the sky. We were both right though – how can that be?

It all comes down to the point of view that we had. You see, I was looking out the west window and he was looking out the east window. It all comes down to perspective. As I have shared my story and given you thoughts to ponder, there would be some agreement, some disagreement and some thoughts that will take longer for you to sort through.

This week, I want to examine some old thoughts and consider some new ways of thinking when it comes to your view, especially as it pertains to beauty.

The beautiful promise given to us is that when we come to Jesus the old is gone and everything is new. This newness is God's view of us. It may take us a little longer to let go of older ways of thinking. But for this week let's look at some ways to help ourselves to look at things as if we are seeing them for the first time.

Thought to ponder

If we have become 'new', what does that mean to the way we begin to see ourselves? What is an old trait that you have held as a belief about yourself that you need to cast off?

Day 72

REFLECTING BACK

History is important. I do a major reflection activity at least twice a year. This is on New Year's Eve or New Year's Day and on my birthday. I record special dates and milestones and I feel these need to be reflected on from time to time.

Remembering is important for us to see the hand of God that has been on our lives. And looking back is a good way to see His faithfulness. In Deuteronomy 6, the commandments were to be not only on the hearts of the people, but they were told, "impress them on your children. Talk about them when you sit at home and when you walk along the road, when you lie down and when you get up." (vs 7)

For New Testament believers, we practice the Lord's Supper to remember the sacrifice that Jesus made for our sins.

Holding on to memories where you may have been hurt would mean a lack of forgiveness towards those who hurt you. It is not a healthy way to reflect. Neither do I mean to continually look back to see what things you have done wrong in the hopes of correcting your path in the future.

A few people refer to the concept of driving down the highway while staring into the rear-view mirror as being an unsafe way to travel. Also, have you ever noticed that when you look at a vehicle, the front window is significantly larger than the rear view mirror? This is a good way to remember that looking back is to be a quick brief look, especially if you are in middle of some form of evaluation.

> **Thought to ponder**
>
> What is your practice and for what purpose do you have a time of reflection? In looking back, what are some times where you can see God's fingerprints in your life?

Day 73

ENVISION

---

*Y*esterday we looked at two points in time where I spend time on those days by looking back. But I also use those times to look forward. Vision casting is often more talked about, but I want to use the word "envision".

Envision is the creative part. The sitting down. Pausing. Thinking hard and if you can, to put your pen to paper and see what your mind creates for what you would like to see going forward.

It is an exciting moment. It can be at the beginning of the year, the beginning of the month, the beginning of the week or even the beginning of the day. We know that each day is a brand-new day. We cannot change the past and the future stretches out before us. All the pages ahead are blank, just waiting to be filled.

Is it okay to admit to a little bit of apprehension? Not in the full fear way but that exciting feeling of the unknown. As we move forward either in the next year of our life or the new year of the calendar, we often set various goals for what we hope to accomplish.

Without this process, we might just wander through life rather than finding and fulfilling the path that God wants for us. Some people have called this self-actualisation. I feel there are stages that we are the best of ourselves.

> ### Thought to ponder
> What practice do you keep regarding vision casting? Take some time to pray and ask Holy Spirit for a view of your future. As you pray, create a plan with purpose and intention for the week ahead.

Day 74

A NEW NAME

When I was born, my parents did not agree on my full name. As the story goes, I was John William until the doctor said that I was a girl. My sister got the family names, being named by both my grandmothers and my mother. There was a young girl, Jill MacKinnon, who use to babysit my older siblings. She was so excited to prepare for the baby shower before my coming. Sadly she died shortly before I was born. My mom asked her mother's permission to call me Jill.

There were two aunts of my father, and he wanted me to be either Barbara Jill or Margaret Jill. In the end the decision of Jill being my first name was finally decided. My mother saw in a magazine a picture of Lake Louise, a beautiful lake in Alberta, and so Louise became my middle name.

Over the years, I have wanted to change my name to Jillian because so many have thought Jill was a short form of Jillian and I got tired of saying "No my name is just Jill." I mentioned it once to my mother who said that my father really loved my being named Jill. And so no changes were made until I was 25 when I took the name of my new husband and became Jill Weatherhead.

In the Bible, both in the Old and New Testament, we see times when names are changed. Mostly it had to do with the idea of a new identity or a change that had happened to them.

Your name is often the most precious to you and your strongest identity. There are those very few people I allow to call me Jilly – the only way to make my name into any form of nick name.

So while I am still Jill, I feel like I should have a new name now as I rediscover who the authentic Jill – the Jill God designed - truly is. Revelation 2 speaks of the fact that to him who overcomes, a new name will be given.

> **Thought to ponder**
> What do you feel about your name and how does it make you see yourself?

Day 75

NEW DIRECTION

For most of my life I feel that I have been living in a transition state. A feeling of "when we get to this point in time then..." The creation of this book is a result of a new direction that I took as 2021 came to an end.

The new direction involved moving forward to being authentically me. I made the big goal as we turned to 2022 to 'step up and step in' to Jill. Not just any Jill. This Jill was going to be the best version so far.

Rather than just chasing her – I was going to be her. Rather than just making dreams for the future – I was going to embrace my dreams.

This pivot from nursing to something new has me taking one step forward, then pausing sometimes mid step. Fear steps in. I fear falling back to the old ways. To giving in to the old because it is familiar. I am reminded that I need to set out specific measurable goals. Markers if you will, that help me move in a more forward direction.

There is no way to know how long I have to live. What I want to do though is to live each day with a purpose. If you are reading this book, then one of my major life goals has been accomplished. If you are feeling a positive shift in your journey towards a better version of yourself and a better understanding of "beauty", then I am rejoicing!

> **Thought to ponder**
>
> Do you believe you are chasing or embracing your dreams? Is there a step you can take today or this week to get one step closer to your dream?

Day 76

THE PURPOSE OF LIFE

I was in a webinar recently and the speaker was addressing the topic "What do you see is your purpose in life?" Her talk went on to teach us how to do a vision board.

The idea of this is that you think of the things that you want to have in your life, and you create a 'board' of images that reflect those dreams for the future.

It is an interesting exercise. A group of us later shared with each other what our 'boards' were and gave a bit of an explanation.

When the pandemic stalled me from doing what I normally did (travel globally doing mission work), it was a time of wondering about my purpose of life. As we came out of that locked-down season, a famous actress Betty White died just short of her 100th birthday. She was reported to have said that she believed her purpose in life was to bring joy and laughter. Life does not stop until we stop having life. I like that.

Years ago, my life was centered around the idea of a career or vocation. I started out as a secretary and then my dream of becoming an RN came true. As a mother of two sons, my purpose of life was very focused on them. While they now are grown men with families of their own, I am reminded by them that I am still needed but my purposes are different now.

Even with my husband, my wife roles shift as his health changes.

Embracing that while a big phase of my life is complete in some sense, I look forward to the next one. And for me I dream of becoming an igniter - sparking beauty! I know there is much that I have accomplished but I also know there is still much I long to do – and to make a difference is one huge goal.

> **Thought to ponder**
>
> Psalm 27 gives us one of the purposes of our life – to serve the Lord. How do our dreams align with this view? Rather than a full vision board, take some time to free your imagination and see if there is one thing you picture of your future life.

Day 77

TIME TO GO DEEPER
JOURNAL ACTIVITY

"I will instruct you and teach you in the way you should go; I will counsel you with my eye upon you." Psalm 32:8 (ESV)

As you conclude this week that has focused on taking a new look, this chapter was originally written the week before New Year's Day. The ideas of newness were surrounded by the reflecting back on the past year and looking ahead to what might be.

The hope we have in Christ is that we are new when we step into faith and believe in Him. Jesus called it being born again (John 3:3). If that is not what you have experienced, I pray that you can see the beauty that is found in making this decision.

Imagine this "the old is past – the new has come" (2 Corinthians 5:14-17).

The wonderful aspect of life is that we don't have to wait. Each day is a new day. Your story is not finished and today is a brand-new blank page for you to fill.

Does this not spark hope and beauty within you?

> ## Read – Reflect – Pray
>
> Psalm 103 (spend extra time on verse 12); Isaiah 1:18; Lamentations 3:22-23

Week 12

FARMING

*"And he told them many things in parables, saying:
"A sower went out to sow. And as he sowed,
some seeds fell along the path, and the birds came
and devoured them. Other seeds fell
on rocky ground, where they did not have much soil,
and immediately they sprang up, since they had
no depth of soil, but when the sun rose,
they were scorched. And since they had no root,
they withered away. Other seeds fell among thorns,
and the thorns grew up and choked them…"
Matthew 13:3-8 (ESV)*

Day 78

HOW DOES YOUR GARDEN GROW?

At the beginning of our journey, together we looked at getting our house in order. Now after many days of study, I thought I would use another analogy to help you in your journey to become the best you that you can be and use one of my favorite parables.

One of the constants we can count on in life is that as there are seasons, they all bring with them a variety of changes. Nature is a great way to see how life moves through seasons. I want to look at a garden and how to have a healthy crop. While there is a great variety of gardens for the purpose of this week, I'm going to look more closely at a vegetable garden. And even more specifically, one that would be planted near a house.

As we look at the garden, it important to remember that while there are times in our lives that we feel that nothing is happening, even in our 'winter' season, life does not stand still. I am here to tell you that in the garden of life, things are always in motion. So, for as long as you inhale and exhale a breath, you not only have something going on inside, but you also have a purpose.

Some people who garden have what is known as a green thumb. I believe that description suits my landlady. I have to admit to not being as successful in previous years. Interestingly though as I work through some of my belief systems, I see some parallels between the lack of growth in the garden and the lack of growth in my life.

So, let's get started on our garden and see where this will take us in our journey and desire to spark our inner beauty. To ignite the light and passion that I know is there inside you!

> **Thought to ponder**
>
> In which season of your life have you seen the most growth? What environmental factors are necessary for seeds to flourish and grow? How does that relate with our lives?

Day 79

HOW TO GET STARTED

It has been interesting for me in my world travels to have gained an understanding when it comes to getting started on a garden. Regardless of where you live, you will have a variety of seasons. For the sake of this writing, we will go with the four main ones that I grew up with – winter, spring, summer, fall.

The writer of Ecclesiastes tells us that there is a season for everything. (Ecclesiastes Chapter 3)

If we really want to see change, we first must be open to some new ideas. This is the season which we are going to call Winter.

In Winter, here in Canada, it feels like things are dormant. The ground is frozen for long periods of time. It seems like the only trees that show true life are those known as 'evergreen' trees.

Are you in Winter right now? Do you feel like your life is dormant?

If you do plan on putting in a garden during that season, you actually need to start now. My landlady has been my guide when it comes to the physical garden. She told me she is always working on her garden. (She has both flower and vegetable gardens.)

She gains gardening knowledge by talking to other friends, looking at magazines, planning out how to make changes to her present situation. Even in this season she is looking at things like Farmer's

Almanac to gain a better understanding of what will be needed. If something in a previous year did not go well, she talks to others to learn from them.

Then lists are made. And the winter months fly by as she determines the size of the garden, how she will plant (from seed or starters), where exactly to plant (too much shade vs too much sun), and even when to plant.

In our winter, as much as we might tend to hibernate, it is actually the time to reach out and seek guidance from others.

> **Thought to ponder**
> How are you during the winter months? Do you find you need more self care than at other seasons?

Day 80

PREPARING THE GARDEN

The next season that comes after winter I think of as Spring. I think of this season as Spring. If you have spent any time reading the Bible, you might be familiar with the story Jesus told of "The Sower and the Seed". Culturally in the time of the story a person would have a sack filled with seed and they would walk along their land spreading it by hand. One of the lessons to learn from this parable is to have hope that some seed would take root, grow, and provide a crop.

I would like to suggest that not everyone is ready to receive the 'seed'. The soil of their life may have been rocky, or thorny, or lacking in essentials of health. It does not mean that the seed cannot be planted in these soils. However, it will take more work on the role of the gardener to ensure growth occurs.

Are you able to evaluate your own personal 'soil'? Is there something lacking so that nutrients are needed before you can receive the 'seed' that will help you grow forward?

One consideration is that if there was a seed that had fallen on soil not conducive to growth, the next action would be transplanting to a more fertile area. How is your environment then? Are there changes that need to be made? Or is it possible you need to be transplanted to a place where you can not only grow but thrive?

> **Thought to ponder**
>
> What is so important about the treatment of soil? How does this relate to the soil in our lives (our hearts)? What did Jesus mean when he talked of the 'good soil' and what does that mean for the way we live our lives?

Day 81

PLANTING STAGE

It is during the planting stage of the garden that this is often when things are exciting. We plant with the expectation of what will happen in a few weeks or months.

If we are diligent, we will prepare the soil to receive the seed or seedling.

The rocks, or the weeds and thorns of the past, are cleared away. Nutrients are often added to the soil.

Interestingly, this is the one stage that most people seem to know the most about. There is a nurturing feeling in the planting of the seed. Just this simple act of putting something into motion.

When you think of seeds in relation to life, it is the idea of sowing and reaping but also it can be seen as a point of renewal. A new seed of thought could lead to a point of regeneration. A rebirth if you will. A newness.

If you are planting a garden, there is even that point in the planting when you find yourself down on your knees, coming face to face with the dirt. The strong scent rising to heighten your sense of smell as the freshness of the dirt is evident in the air.

Planting is a hard season in the garden. It usually takes a lot of physical effort. Some people even do it in stages to not get too tired or sore from the bending and kneeling that is often necessary.

The seed could be seen similar to a spark. It is small. It has the capacity to grow into something very large if nurtured well.

And at the end of the planting, a feeling of hope arises. A hope of something beautiful that will come in the not-too-distant future. The question of a harvest is yet to be seen, but the hope for one remains strong at this point in time.

For me the seeds represent the new ideas, the dreams, the hopes of a future.

> **Thought to ponder**
>
> On this journey so far what are some seeds – some new beliefs – that you have discovered so far on this journey? What will be some important steps to take to nurture these new thoughts to ensure they are deeply imbedded in your belief system?

Day 82

NOW THAT THE SEED IS SOWN WHAT IS NEXT?

———————

As Spring ends and we move into Summer, the seeds have been planted and now is a time of waiting.

Have you ever planted something and waited for signs of 'life'? Even if the seed package said, "takes 3 weeks to germinate," did you find yourself out in the garden checking to see that first sprout?

You can't rush it. Seeds take time to grow.

And it is the same with us as well. Maybe by now in this 90-day journey you have made a discovery about yourself. Maybe you are still pondering some of what has been said, trying to decide if it pertains to you.

Spring – the trees are blooming. The robins have returned. The weather warms. The snow disappears. Even the unexpected snow that might come one more time is only a mild frustration because we have the hope of Summer.

As these two seasons blend and shift, it is easy to have a sense of 'new'. At the same time is the waiting. And the unknowing if what we planted will even sprout and bring life.

Again, this is not a dormant time of waiting. There is still work to be done.

Weeding. Watering. Feeding.

Depending on your garden, it might need to be protected from things that seek to destroy.

Thought to ponder

What are some benefits of the weeding, watering, feeding in this phase? How does this relate to the next steps you will need to take when these 90 days are complete?

Day 83

SUMMER IS HERE!

In my opinion, Summer is the shortest season of the Canadian year. I grew up listening to a song about the lazy, hazy, crazy days of summer! Where I live in the Northern Hemisphere, the days are longer. I must admit to this being the best part of summer.

I am eager to get up in the morning and get outside. To feel the sun on my face. To listen to the various sounds of summer.

Beauty is no longer sought, because it is experienced.

A quick walk around the neighborhood opens the senses to the coming alive sights and sounds. Take a walk on a path in nature and again you will see it. Open your eyes to it. Let the light come in and warm the coldness that you have previously felt.

And your garden? Now begins the uncurling of the tiny sprout that seems to grow before your very eyes. The little sprout pushes up through the dirt and within a short period of time there is even a flower that blooms.

Beauty. It is discovered. It is seen. It is felt. It is known.

Thought to ponder

How do you feel in your soul when nature puts on her best during the summer season? What is some fruit you have seen in your life?

Day 84

TIME TO GO DEEPER
JOURNAL ACTIVITY

The Lord will open to you his good treasury, the heavens, to give the rain to your land in its season and to bless all the work of your hands. Deuteronomy 28:12 (ESV)

And now comes the season known as Fall. The harvest is the part that will move you forward.

It does not mean the end. The days here in Canada do get shorter. The weather turns colder. The knowing of winter coming. But we do not lose hope. We recognize that there are seasons of life.

Let's recap then. Are you in Winter? Is your fire barely an ember?

Are you in Spring? There is a small spark, but just barely a flame.

Perhaps you find yourself in Summer with a full-on fire that ignites all around you.

Or is it now Fall, and you are seeing the harvest. The work of your hands shows, and you stand with confidence heading into the ever-changing seasons.

The final thought for this week is this: What happens to your heart? your confidence? your beauty? As you move through the seasons of life?

> **Read – Reflect – Pray**
>
> Matthew 13; Galatians 6:9; James 3:18; John 15:5

Week 13

COMING TO THE END

*I am sure of this, that He who started
a good work in you will carry it on to
completion until the day of Christ Jesus.
Philippians 1:6 (CSB)*

Day 85

COMING TO THE END OF THE JOURNEY

If you have been in Canada and you have driven across the prairies, the lights of the city of Regina get you excited even though they are quite away off in the distance. You know that if that is your resting spot, it is now imaginable that you will make it to your destination.

We have almost completed our 90 days of looking deeper and considering what it will take to spark beauty not only from within ourselves but also how to spread this concept to others who are also in need of this awakening – this fire.

It seems fitting that we started by walking through our house, getting it in order first. And then that we end with the view of a garden. Planting seeds for future growth perhaps not just in this present season.

But this is just the end of our journey for these 90 days. In many ways we are just getting started. Let's take a few more days to look at what we might still need to do in the days, months and years to come.

> **Thought to ponder**
>
> Do we see a difference now in the house we got in order at the start of this journey? Take a moment to consider some of the 'ah ha' moments as we moved through these days together. What is your number one takeaway?

Day 86

A DISTANCE TRAVELED

There have been many days that we have just traveled, not pausing long enough or perhaps we needed to have taken a different road or some time off the journey. And if that is your story, be encouraged that even that being the case you are here now. Your awareness has been at least heightened if only a little bit (for some) or perhaps like a lightening bolt (for others).

Regardless of the journey, I can tell you that there has always been beauty. In me. Around me.

There were times though when all I could see was the dark and the rain. It reminds me of my first rainy season in Papua New Guinea. The constant rain and cloudy sky had a direct impact on my spirit. It was already difficult to deal with the adjustment to living in a jungle. The rain was the one more thing that brought me to my knees.

I remember asking God to help me. I did not need a full sky of blue but just a little peek here and there each day.

For the month of February 1998, every day that prayer was answered. It became something that my sons started to watch for and would interrupt me if I was reading or not paying attention and they would say "Mom come quickly, God's blue sky is appearing" as they pointed up to the little peak in the clouds. They told the kids in the village and soon that was what all the kids watched for and marvelled when it happened. I can still hear them calling out, "White woman white woman the big God opened the sky. Come quickly and look."

My request to God started a spark - that grew - and others were ignited. Remember the camp song? "It only takes a spark to get a fire going". On the very last day of February there was the most beautiful rainbow. One of the elders of the village said, "God put that there for you."

Even to this day, I find that when I look, I see God's promises – His "fingerprints" as my son Glen would often say. And there is almost always someone that randomly says, "this is something sent to you by God".

This is the spark - the hope - that makes us want to run and tell everyone - look and see the beauty!

> **Thought to ponder**
> Would you take a moment right now and go look in the mirror? Is anything different?

Day 87

COME OUT FROM HIDING

Have you played a game of hide and seek? I used to as a teenager and sometimes I would find the best spot so that the others would call out to me to come out from hiding. In the song "This little light of mine" there is the verse that we are not supposed to hide our light.

In thinking about hiding, there are times that I decided it was safer to just stay hidden. And here are two thoughts on why I felt this was the way to be:

The first is that someone told me to hide. At some point in the past, I was told, or I believed that letting my full light shine -- allowing the inner beauty that is in creation to freely flow - was not acceptable. It would be considered vain to consider that you had beauty.

The other is that someone told me that I was not beautiful, and I had not beauty at all. Not even on the inside. And on that day, I decided to hide deep within myself the real me. To keep her hidden as a way of protection, only letting her out on a very rare occasion and for only a select few people – the ones who loved me unconditionally.

We have spent together twelve weeks looking at all aspects of beauty. I would love to know if you are willing to come out from hiding in the shadows. To put your light out like the city on a hill. To rise and shine and give God the glory of creating you.

It may take more than just this study, but I have been praying for you. Praying that at a minimum there is a small crack. A new belief and a little spark.

> ### Thought to ponder
> What is it about yourself you are hiding, afraid to show the world? Is there one step you can take today to come out from under the covers? To shine?

Day 88

BEAUTY WITH CONFIDENCE

_____

As we conclude our 90 days, I can say that there is a confidence regarding how I feel with this idea of inner beauty. I have to admit that I was a bit fearful to even say that. Would it not sound like I was arrogant? Vain? Proud?

I do not believe so. I want to believe that while I have grown to be self-aware that it is different to being self-absorbed. In my newfound confidence, there is no need to compete with others, but instead I can share my strengths and help those around who may be struggling. I am learning that even as I age, I still have worth, value and purpose in life.

Slowly but steadily I am learning that with my eyes fully focused on God then I cannot get lost. By letting Him create the map for me to follow then I will never be completely lost. I know from His promises that he goes before, beside and behind me.

I can be the authentic Jill.

I will be honest. In this 90 days while I do believe I have grown in awareness, and even started to step up and step into the woman I was meant to be, I still struggle.

Thought to ponder

What will be the difference now in your life if you stand with confidence of who you are?

Day 89

HAVE YOU SEEN THE SUNRISE?

And now, just as you accepted Christ Jesus as your Lord, you must continue to follow him. Let your roots grow down into him, and let your lives be built on him. Then your faith will grow strong in the truth you were taught, and you will overflow with thankfulness. Colossians 2:6-7 (NLT)

One of the benefits I have had over the years of working night shifts is seeing the sunrise. No matter what type of night it had been, there is a calm and reassurance that life is OK as I drive home, and the sun breaks over the horizon.

A new day has dawned.

From the ridge near where I live, I often can see the mountains in that last bit of my drive home. As the sun stretches it is like a spotlight. Majesty.

Creation. What is more beautiful than that?

And if you don't know it - you are very much a part of that beauty.

That is the beauty I want everyone to experience.

Perhaps you have done these days and you feel like there are more questions than answers. Or perhaps you did these 90 days, and you feel renewed, reborn, ready to take on the next 90 plus days.

Thought to Ponder

Take a few moments to pray and then I want you to stand and make a positive declaration about your life and your future.

Day 90

HELLO EVERYONE! I'M HOME!

One of the best parts of living away from my childhood home was taking a trip to go back and visit. As I burst through the doors and said, "Hello everyone – it's me I'm home".

Now everyone was not always a lot of people. But I would soon do the rounds to everyone, and it was all hugs and kisses and 'we've missed you'.

It is what I picture it will be like when I get to heaven, actually. I will run through those doors and yell to everyone "Hello everyone. I'm home!"

And that is our celebration today!

We started out together on a journey. A journey for me to share with you a bit of my story in the hopes that it would open your eyes. To take off the blinders put there by society and some of the lies that may have been spoken over you. To open the window shades that may have been blocking the light from shining outwards from your inner being.

I have shared a lot of my faith in God and truly it is His faithfulness towards me that has brought me safely through the over six decades of my life to this point. And I have the confidence in knowing He will continue to be as faithful as the sun rises in the East and sets in the West.

We have climbed the mountain. We stand now on the peak looking out into the world around us.

I feel the exhilaration of the climb – of the journey - and want to extend my arms high into the air and shout:

> *"How beautiful on the mountains are the feet of those who bring good news, who proclaim peace, who bring good tidings, who proclaim salvation, who say to Zion, "Your God reigns!" Isaiah 52:7 (ESV)*

THIS IS NOT THE END - IT IS IN FACT A NEW BEGINNING

Congratulations on 90 days of journeying with me as together we explored various thoughts and ideas, learning to find ways to spark and ignite beauty – within and without.

This book has been a journey for me that I actually started years ago, without even knowing what it would become. I do believe we are all on a journey. And I'm so thankful for all the times in my life that I have seen glimpses of beauty to bring me to this moment in time.

Recently I was reminded of the Old Testament story found in Genesis 35 when Jacob loses the love of his life – Rachel. It was pointed out to me that it was Jacob who buried Rachel. A few verses later it says that Israel moved on. This is a beautiful picture of transformation really. At this moment of pain, this man – formally known as Jacob – stepped into the called life he was to live – as Israel. In the same way, I hope for you to be so transformed. Perhaps even give yourself a new name. The value of our name was discussed already so I will stay with Jill but in my heart, I believe "Jilly" (youthful, playful spirit) reflects the real me. The apple of my father's eyes. And my Father's eyes.

There is much discussion in this book about God and my belief of His faithfulness. It would take another book to share all the times He has shown Himself to me. If you do not know Him, then it is my prayer this book will not just spark the beauty within you, but it will also draw you to a desire to learn and know Him.

Finally for me? I truly believe my beauty is when I have my Father's eyes – of compassion, kindness, goodness, mercy and above all – love.

I leave you with this thought, hope and prayer to be true in your life.

> *For now we see in a mirror dimly, but then face to face. Now I know in part; then I shall know fully, even as I have been fully known. I Corinthians 13:12 (ESV)*

ABOUT THE AUTHOR

Jill Weatherhead is married to Dr. Norm and they make their home in Calgary, AB. For over 25 years they have been missionaries with Pioneer Bible Translators, working primarily in Papua New Guinea, but also doing a shorter term in Tanzania. Their two sons are married and have given her 5 amazing grandchildren!

In the Fall of 2022, she left her nursing career behind to embark on her mission to redefine beauty - to spark beauty in others. It is her passion to help other women understand and grow in the revelation of their inner and outer beauty.

Manufactured by Amazon.ca
Bolton, ON

31536004R00125